All the best!

Bill Hermann

Giving the Gift of a Career

A ROADMAP FOR INDIVIDUALLY FOCUSED STAFF DEVELOPMENT

More Praise for Giving the Gift of a Career

"Bill Hermann's book delivers timeless and practical advice for career builders and career seekers based on the enduring principle: One size fits one person. This advice is delivered in a usable format with tools that readers can implement right away. *Giving the Gift of a Career* is steeped in the philosophies of Plante Moran, a much-admired and successful professional services firm. For those curious about the secrets of its longevity these 90-plus years, the book gives a powerful insight."

—Allan Gilmour, former Wayne State University president and Ford Motor Company vice chair

"This small tome says it all! This hands-on book with checklists and questions in each chapter is all about investing in your staff to promote their personal and professional growth, which translates into higher staff morale, happier clients, and a better bottom line. Bill and his partners at Plante Moran realized long ago that for individuals to achieve success, they require personalized attention and an environment that nurtures them along the way. If your firm is struggling with recruiting and retention, this is the book you need to read."

—August Aquila, CEO of AQUILA Global Advisors, LLC, international consultant to professional services firms, author, and keynote speaker

"In this book, Bill Hermann captures the fundamental ethos that has made Plante Moran one of the most successful professional services firms and one which Broad Spartans clamor to work for. Mentoring, delegation, and teamwork are well-known personnel management concepts that are key to recruiting and retaining strong talent, yet many organizations struggle to ensure that these concepts are firmly embedded in their culture and fabric. This book underscores the importance of recognizing that talent is best developed and nurtured if one takes a 'one size fits one person' approach. A simple, yet powerful, concept, especially as the millennials and Gen Zers become the dominant part of the workforce. This book offers all readers keen insights into everyday lessons on leadership that are easy to implement and can have a long-lasting positive impact for any organization."

—Sanjay Gupta, the Eli and Edythe L. Broad Dean of Michigan State University's Broad College of Business

"When EKS&H first began discussions with Plante Moran, we had a lot in common, including core values and cultural alignment. This book by Bill Hermann spells out in clear terms the reasons why we were in synch. He has written an outstanding playbook with hands-on guidance on how to develop your most important resource: your people."

—Robert Hottman, Plante Moran partner and one of the original founders of EKS&H of Colorado, which joined Plante Moran in 2018

Giving the Gift of a Career

A ROADMAP FOR INDIVIDUALLY FOCUSED STAFF DEVELOPMENT

Bill Hermann

MOMENTUM BOOKS, LLC
TROY, MICHIGAN

Published by Momentum Books, LLC, a subsidiary of HOUR Media, LLC

5750 New King Drive, Suite 100
Troy, Michigan 48098
momentumbooks.com

Printed and bound in the U.S.A.

ISBN-13: 978-1-938018-20-6
ISBN-10: 1938018206
Library of Congress Control Number: 2020905262

Illustrations by Lillian Noga, Katie Huang, and Ken Cendrowski

Contents

Personalized Development 'For All'

By Michael C. Bush, CEO, Great Place to Work®

Bill Hermann has it right.

These days, developing your staff has to be personal. And personalized.

It has to be about caring leaders and organizations that tailor career growth plans to the needs and wishes of individual employees.

How else do you expect to bring out the best in millennials and Gen Zers, who've grown up in an era of personalization?

How else do you expect to bring out the best in anyone these days, when we are all living with individualized Facebook feeds, Netflix accounts, and workout programs?

What's more, when leaders give the gift of a customized development experience, employees reciprocate. They give more and they stick with you. They aren't constantly updating their LinkedIn profiles. And when headhunters call, they don't respond.

This book is full of great ideas for customizing staff development. And it is full of inspiring stories from Bill's longtime employer, accounting and professional services firm Plante Moran. Bill and the crew at Plante Moran are heroes in my eyes. For more than 20 years, they have earned a place on the "100 Best Companies to Work For" ranking that we publish with *Fortune* magazine. That's not an easy accomplishment. It means Plante Moran's people have felt great enough about their workplace experience that for two decades they consistently have given it top marks on our Trust Index Employee Survey.

The great scores and the 100 Best honors aren't surprising when you consider this fact: Plante Moran has one of the highest concentrations of what we call "For All Leaders."

For All Leaders create positive experiences for virtually everyone on their team, no matter who they are or what they do for the organization. For All Leaders have traits such as humility, the ability to build bonds of trust with and among team members, and a focus on the bigger purpose.

For All Leaders also deliver the kind of personalized employee development called for today. When Bill Hermann encourages managers to build caring relationships with staffers, when he suggests spending 80% of performance management meetings looking forward and just 20% looking backward, when he calls for thoughtfully pairing up junior employees with collaborators who will teach but not overwhelm, he's talking about practicing For All Leadership.

He's also talking about eliminating much of the fear that debilitates employees and companies. Personalized development plans created by For All Leaders make people less afraid of being left in the dust with outdated skills in a fast-moving economy. And less afraid of being stuck in a deadening job with no room to advance.

We hear a lot today about people's anxiety about automation and artificial intelligence stealing jobs. Our research into tens of thousands of employee comments found something surprising. We learned that people aren't afraid of a robot taking their jobs — they are afraid of being treated like a robot. That is, they are concerned about managers who fail to see their unique talents and how those can be developed.

People with For All Leaders don't have those worries. On the contrary, they often can't wait to see how technological advances can help them and their teams move forward. Indeed, we see hard evidence that For All Leadership, with its focus on personalized bonds with team members, pays off. Our study of 10,000 managers and 75,000 employees discovered that indicators for productivity, agility, retention, and innovation increase dramatically for teams led by For All Leaders. Compared to teams managed by less inclusive supervisors, teams headed by For All Leaders saw our indicator for innovation jump 325%.

When leaders listen to people's dreams and invite them to bring their best ideas for improving the organization, employees find ways to contribute that executive teams can't even imagine. These "Innovation By All" cultures act more like a flock of birds, where any one employee can steer the organization toward a new opportunity or away from an emerging threat.

What you get is agility far beyond what's possible in top-down, machine-like companies that dictate how people must be trained based on fixed guidelines.

The emerging economy of digital disruption will make such rigid and impersonal company structures extinct.

Not only will old-school, industrial cultures fall behind, but they won't be able to attract or retain key talent. Millennials now make up the majority of employees, and our research shows they describe their ideal leader as deeply concerned with their long-term growth. At certified-great workplaces like Plante Moran — that is, companies with large numbers of For All Leaders — 81% of millennials plan a long future at their company. At U.S. companies overall, the figure is just 44%.

I encourage you to soak up all the good ideas from Bill and Plante Moran in this book. And I thank them for sharing their personal, personalized approach to people development.

As I said, Bill's got it right.

A Word from the Author

Over the years, I've observed that staff tend to fall into three career trajectories. There's the "Shooting Star," whose career is marked by early success. They seem to accomplish more in their first years with the firm than the average staff member. Their career would resemble an arc with a steep rise at the front end and an apex a few years out. Next is "Steady Eddie," who makes even, continuous strides over time while advancing at a steady pace. This person's trajectory would appear to be more of a straight-line graph, rising from the bottom left of the chart toward the top right. And then there's the "Late Bloomer," the person who starts slowly and takes some time to find their footing.

But you can't be fooled by first impressions. You might hope a Shooting Star will last forever, but, most likely, their trajectory will level off someday. A Late Bloomer might just need some time to hit their stride.

It takes time, observation, and patience to determine the true potential of each staff member in your organization. The process of working with staff members and helping them thrive in their careers is the focus of this book.

In 2001, management guru Jim Collins said, "The single biggest constraint on the success of any organization is the ability to get and to hang on to enough of the right people."

Those words from his groundbreaking work, *Good to Great*, still resonate nearly 20 years later. When it comes to staff, senior leaders everywhere are wrestling with the same challenges: attracting talented people, leveraging their skills to optimize their productivity, and creating an environment (whether they work remotely, in an office setting, or any combination of the two) that encourages their engagement and motivation so they stay.

As I look back at my almost 50-year career, what profoundly impresses me is how unique each and every one of us is. Every Shooting Star, Steady Eddie, and Late Bloomer has their own special personalities, working styles, and personal histories.

As a staff developer, I realized that for individuals to achieve success, they require attention on a personal level and an environment that's willing to nurture each person along their journey.

This awareness didn't hit me all at once — much of what I learned about staff development was the result of trial and error and real-world experiences. For example, an early lesson came when I was a young manager assigned to lead the firm's startup office in Ann Arbor, Michigan. My objectives were to build the business and leverage the skill set of the staff.

The early years were a bit rough. The office was growing, but we had a reputation as a demanding place to work. Clearly, this was a challenge because what good is growth if you don't have the staff members to support the work? It took me a while to recognize that we needed to create an environment where individual staff could be nurtured in their development while contributing to the success of a dynamic new office.

So, we implemented a number of new approaches to staff development. These included spending more time walking the halls, expressing interest for each staff member, and making personal connections along the way. Another adjustment was to leverage our team structure by assigning most of the newer staff members to teams led by managers with strong interpersonal skills. These managers had a warm and collegial approach that created a welcoming environment for the younger staff. As these staff developed their skills, they were introduced to other process-focused managers who involved them in projects that taught them the organizational skills necessary to become good client servers.

The combination of these managers and a commitment to the development needs of each individual helped improve the image of the office from a demanding workplace to a dynamic environment where you could learn, grow, have fun, and develop both personally and professionally. The office continued to grow, and we benefited from having more staff members who were attracted to the environment and wanted to work there.

As I reflect back on these and other personal experiences while developing staff, I realize that I had to discover an awful lot about me — who I am, what I'm good at, what I like or don't like, and what I had to accomplish if I were to be successful professionally and personally. I've always wanted to know what makes things tick, and that includes having a genuine interest in helping and growing people and supporting their future success. I've been empowered and motivated by the knowledge that if I can retain more people, they'll have time to develop in their roles, which will support the growth of the business. So, it was important to understand what would make a difference to each person with whom I interacted. It required suggestions and observations that were tailored to each situation and each person based on their unique needs. In other words, *staff development worked best when one size fit one person.*

At Plante Moran, I interacted with scores of professionals, and it's clear that I learned as much or more from them as I was able to convey in my role as supervisor, coach, or mentor. This book is my attempt to share what I have learned.

In Chapter 1, we'll explore how an individualized approach to staff development supports and sustains the life of that business. If your organization has good talent, it's a shame to waste it. In Chapter 2, we'll discuss the importance of self-awareness, offering several tools that help advisees better understand their strengths, weaknesses, and personal and professional preferences.

In Chapter 3, we'll dig into the ever-important question of balance, and we'll offer techniques to balance personal, professional, and community pursuits. Chapter 4 explores the stages of staff development, from new hire to experienced and trusted leader. Along the way, we'll discuss the value of experiential learning and the benefit of timely feedback to help advisees in their developmental journey. We'll also discuss the essential value of asking questions, and how the answers to those questions can fuel staff development. Chapter 5 breaks down the benefits to be gained from a productive mentoring experience, while Chapter 6 focuses on an essential attribute of leadership development: delegation.

Finally, in Chapter 7 we'll discuss business development, and we'll offer hands-on tools that can help staff members embrace the business development/sales challenge, whether it's in their comfort zone or not.

Included along the way are some words of guidance, advice, and lessons I acquired during my career. So, it's essentially my Plante Moran inheritance I seek to share with you here. I hope it helps you as you grow and progress as a staff developer and professional. I also hope once you have the opportunity to influence others, you'll pass along what you've learned and pay it forward.

—Bill Hermann, March 2020

I have often told this story to illustrate that no success comes without work and a struggle.

The Butterfly Story

A man found a cocoon of a butterfly. One day, a small opening appeared. He sat and watched the butterfly for several hours as it struggled to force its body through that little hole. Then it seemed to stop making progress. It appeared as if it had gotten as far as it could, and it could go no further.

So, the man decided to help the butterfly. He took a pair of scissors and snipped off the remaining bit of the cocoon.

The butterfly then emerged easily. But it had a swollen body and small, shriveled wings.

The man continued to watch the butterfly because he expected that, at any moment, the wings would enlarge and expand to be able to support the body, which would contract in time.

Neither happened! In fact, the butterfly spent the rest of its life crawling around with a swollen body and shriveled wings. It never was able to fly.

What the man, in his kindness and haste, didn't understand was that the restricting cocoon and the struggle required for the butterfly to get through the tiny opening were nature's way of forcing fluid from the body of the butterfly into its wings so that it would be ready for flight once it achieved its freedom from the cocoon.

Sometimes struggles are exactly what we need in our lives. Remember, nature needs no help, nor interference. There are processes in life — things we all go through. The struggles are part of our journey and are preparing us for what awaits. They are preparing us to fly.

—Author unknown

Gratitude and Thanks

First and above all, thank you to my wife, Sue, for the support, cheerleading, and patience she has generously provided these 50-some years. Thanks also to our children, grandchildren, nieces, nephews, and the extended Hermann family. I'm grateful for my parents, Ed and Anna Mae Hermann, who gave me an example to follow, encouragement, and an occasional swift kick.

Thank you to the Plante Moran family including clients, team partners, buddies, mentors, and mentees whom I've been fortunate to observe and who taught me so much. We all owe a deep debt to Frank Moran, Bob Petz, and others who started the "grand experiment" that became the cultural foundation for the firm and that's been carried forward by Bill Bufe and others.

Thank you to the friends and colleagues from my nearly 50 years at Plante Moran who shared, showed, and led the way, as well as these current and former Plante Moran staff who contributed stories and anecdotes: Frank Audia, Richard Brehler, Gary Caranci, Dan Chewning, Jeff Dolowy, Kathy Downey, Kim Doyle, Michelle Goss, Steve Gravenkemper, Cathy Hare, Robert Hartman, Ken Hermann, Blake Jobkar, Gordon Krater, Ken Kunkel, Chris McCoy, Raj Patel, Jim Proppe, Bruce Shapiro, Mike Swartz, Craig Thornton, and Dan Trotta.

Thank you to Jeff Antaya, Mindy Kroll, Andrew Patterson, and Michelle Welsh from the Plante Moran marketing team for your help framing many of these ideas, and particularly Teresa McAlpine, who provided the energy to document these concepts for future generations. I also appreciate the contribution of author and attorney Steve Lehto, who contributed copy, ideas, and perspective to this book.

Thank you to Steve Gerhardt for providing input, and to Rob Pasick and the members of our "unsuccessful" retirement readiness support group. I very much appreciate the lively forums that allowed us to share ideas, float random concepts, and plan for our future selves.

Finally, thanks to Robert Scheuermann, esteemed former English teacher at Catholic Central High School. I apologize for any dangling participles.

"When planning for a year, plant corn. When planning for a decade, plant trees. When planning for life, train and educate people."

—Chinese Proverb

"The saddest thing is when someone decides they are going to leave, and we didn't even know they were unhappy."

—Plante Moran partner

CHAPTER ONE

A Roadmap for Staff Development

It's Monday morning and you arrive at the office early. You're in high spirits because, in a couple of hours, your team will meet with a new client, a prestigious organization whose work you've been trying to win for months. The new client is an ideal match for your team's capabilities, and if this initial project is successful, there's the prospect of more work in the future.

Your enthusiasm fades when your star performer arrives. One look at her face tells you something isn't right. "I won't be able to go on the client call today," she tells you, regretfully. "I've accepted another position at another firm. My husband and I discussed it all weekend, and it wasn't an easy decision, but…"

As she continues talking, a million thoughts race through your mind. What about the client meeting? Who's ready to step in and replace her? What can you offer to get her to stay? Why didn't she tell you she was unhappy and interviewing elsewhere?

This staffing scenario is common in business today. Managers in every type of organization are being caught flat-footed when key staff members depart and they have to manage the fallout. Not only are managers losing the brainpower of their experienced staff, but client relationships may also be jeopardized, and the remaining staff may be overburdened and unprepared to step in. Then there's the cost of replacing the departed staff member, including recruiting, hiring costs, and training, not to mention the productivity drain until the new staff member becomes proficient. In dollars and cents, it's estimated that the cost to hire a replacement amounts to as much as 90–100% of the staff member's annual salary.

There are any number of reasons for voluntary turnover — staff members who leave of their own volition, not asked to leave because of a layoff or performance issues. The Work Institute conducted exit interviews with departing staff recently, and their reasons included career development (22%), work-life balance (12%), manager behavior (11%), compensation and benefits (9%), and well-being (9%).

The fact that more money offered elsewhere is not the number-one reason for staff departures is a wake-up call for organizations that want to retain good talent. Improving retention is largely within your control! That's why businesses are adopting workplace engagement initiatives. They recognize that being a great place to work is good for their staff members and their bottom line. As evidence, companies that have been on *Fortune*'s "100 Best Companies to Work For" list have three times the revenue growth of companies not on the list (source: Great Place to Work).

Not every business is focused on improving the working environment for its staff, but many are still successful and thriving. For managers and staff in those organizations, the mere notion of a team-centric culture and work environment may be foreign, off-kilter, or just not applicable. Even in organizations that pride themselves on being great places to work, there are managers and supervisors who minimize "all that culture stuff." Here are examples of attitudes that might sound similar to the philosophy at your organization:

- If you're not sitting at your computer, you're not working.
- Working at home on a Saturday is flextime.
- Millennials just need to be "trained" to be productive.
- It's the job of the individual to pull themselves up by their own bootstraps.
- Collaboration takes time away from production.
- Staff development is HR's job.

If these are the attitudes at your organization, don't stop reading. I've seen managers implement the suggestions outlined in this book within their own teams in challenging environments, and their staff members grew their skills and loved working for that manager, and others were clamoring to get in on the action and join that team. Who knows? You may start a mini-cultural movement that will lead to long-term changes.

Advisors who recognize talent can help staff find their right place.

"Early in my career, I was working as an auditor, and, honestly, while I liked what I was doing, it was not my sweet spot," says Andrew. His advisors and several of the firm leaders recognized he had strong technical skills and was a good people person, so they approached him about transferring to one of the internal teams, a group that could use help on both fronts. Andrew was open to the change and moved to the new department, where he thrived on the detail that was required and embraced being accountable for developing his new team. He worked with a number of leaders in that group and ultimately became a partner himself, and he credits the advice of half a dozen advisors who counseled him along the way. They encouraged him to soak up as much knowledge as he could, and were candid with him when they felt he wasn't quite ready for the next step. "I didn't envision that I would get that far when I was younger, but I was smart enough to figure out that I should go toward what I enjoyed and try to be the best at what I did."

Staff development is highly valuable now as millennials exert their influence in the workforce. Millennials are projected to be 75% of the global workforce by 2025, and savvy organizations are paying close attention to their needs. As a group, millennials have very different ideals and values than their predecessors, and studies have shown that they're not blindly loyal to the organization that hired them. Instead, they develop loyalty to an organization through interaction with coaches and mentors that provide them opportunities for professional development and growth. Further, they value coaching, mentoring, and experiential learning far above classrooms or e-learning. Some of the practices we'll describe in this book align well with the increasingly millennial workforce.

Regardless of generation and style, staff development will benefit any organization. For example, Plante Moran has one of the lowest voluntary turnover rates among accounting firms and has been recognized nationally and internationally for its culture. In general, the firm's focus on staff development has lowered turnover, which means less spending on hiring and retraining. It's also increased staff stability and goodwill for the firm.

Plante Moran has long been defined by a culture that focuses on the well-being of staff. The firm's founding fathers developed the "Wheel of Progress" that begins and ends with good staff. *Good staff perform good work. Good work attracts good clients. Good clients are willing to pay good fees. Good fees allows us to pay good wages. Good wages attract good staff.*

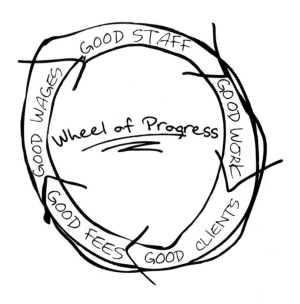

The business case for a staff-focused organizational culture is shown in Plante Moran's "High Touch" system. Each new staff member is assigned to a team led by a partner in the firm. New hires also get a "buddy" — a slightly more experienced peer who provides help and advice. Buddies are invaluable "Sherpas" for new hires trying to learn their way around a new organization. The team partner-buddy combo is supported by practices that include recruiting and hiring individuals with the right skill set; coaching; mentoring; and providing training, formal performance management, and recognition. This "High Touch" system leads naturally to higher staff morale. The morale improvements lead to lower turnover, better teamwork, and happier clients. While these investments all benefit the firm and the staff, happier clients result in a better bottom line for the firm. A better bottom line allows the firm to reinvest in its culture while enjoying higher profits.

"HIGH TOUCH" SYSTEM

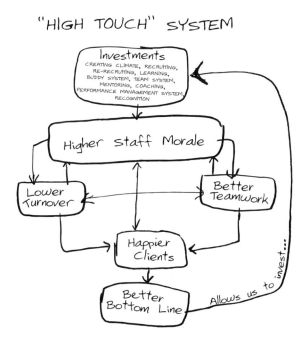

Well-defined performance management and training are key components to support the effectiveness of the "High Touch" system. These formal systems demystify performance expectations, clarify competency definitions, and set criteria for promotions. Equally important is a compensation system that promotes fairness, defines success, and enables individuals to contribute and share in the profitability and growth of the entity.

But a well-defined HR system can't do it alone. It's critical for team leaders and supervisors to commit to support the develop-

During a mentoring session, I was getting to know a new partner, and she was talking about her children and their sports activities. I asked what seemed to be a fairly straightforward question, "How often are you able to attend their games?" and she burst into tears. That simple question helped crystallize a key issue that was bothering her and she was struggling to address. We made it clear that she didn't have to choose between her work and her family life. Then we worked with her to strike the right balance so she could fulfill her tasks at the firm and also be able to attend her family events. Her actions included more delegating, learning to say "no," and carefully selecting the assignments she would accept.

ment of each and every team member. How? By helping each individual understand how they fit within the organization; how they are performing; and what they should do to adjust, refocus, energize, or maintain their efforts. Paying attention to the individual staff member, building relationships with them, listening, coaching, and mentoring are all part of this dynamic.

Individually focused staff development

In a "High Touch" system, each staff member receives highly individualized staff development attention. Why this focus on the individual? Because everyone comes to work with a different mix of strengths, areas for improvement, and personal experiences; in other words, every individual is a "unique piece of clay." We'll delve into individual differences in the self-awareness chapter, but the lesson for the advisor is clear: Staff members who receive individualized guidance and direction from their advisors and supervisors benefit from approaches that are tailored to them — one size does not fit all.

Staff development is not to be confused with training programs to educate staff about the skills necessary to do their jobs. Individually focused staff development helps them reach their ultimate potential by leveraging consistent input from an advisor.

While you can tailor staff development techniques for each individual, not everyone is destined to become a star. Some may not progress as far as others. Individual coaching may highlight the fact that a person may not be a good fit for their role, which could mean they'll need to leave the organization. Or, it could point them toward a different career path.

In our experience we have seen instances where individualized coaching resulted in people deciding to leave their profession altogether. Some joined the ministry, others went to medical school, and in one case, a staff member decided she'd be happiest driving the Oscar Mayer Wienermobile. However, most people who receive individual attention as part of their staff development will improve, and even those who improve only incrementally will be better for it — and so will the organization.

The role of the advisors

The success of the staff development process depends on the trusting relationship between the advisor/supervisor and the advisee/staff person and the effectiveness of communication between them. We can't stress enough that the foundation for effective staff development is built when the advisor takes the time to show authentic interest in the person they're supervising and not just their career progress. Some advisors may be reluctant to spend the time, or they may not be good at it. But the benefits to be gained for the individual performer, for the team, and for the "good work" that will result are worth the effort. In the Appendix, we offer some "re-recruiting" questions that advisors can ask themselves about the people on their team. The answers to these questions are powerful indicators about a staff member's allegiance to the organization, and an advisor who knows these answers could prevent unexpected departures that can be so threatening to the successful functioning of the organization's teams.

The role of the staff person/advisee

Individually focused staff development is not passive for either party; it requires effort from both the advisor and the advisee. The advisor's role is to be there as a guide, but the advisee will be the one making the effort to execute and take on the responsibility for doing so. In fact, the advisee has the primary responsibility to execute the plan and create the results. A supervisor who has a reputation as a great staff developer has said, "Staff development isn't something that we give you. It requires your full and complete commitment."

This guide offers alternatives that allow advisors and their advisees to create individually tailored staff development journeys. The ultimate goal is to maximize an individual's strengths and address their areas for improvement.

The staff development process is not one-and-done. There will be discussions that are formal and informal. (In fact, we believe the greatest impact can happen in informal settings.) Advisors will work with their advisees to set focused goals and hold those staff accountable. They'll also identify experiential learning opportunities and projects where their advisees will work alone or in a team environment. The process expects advisees to spend time in self-reflection about their skills, and it requires — no, *demands* — candid evaluations from the advisor about performance. The process can create discomfort, but the discomfort is constructive. Bottom line: It takes time and effort to leverage the unique skills of an individual and maximize their potential, but the rewards are more than enough to make up for the investment.

However, not all rewards are monetary. Leaders need to recognize that staff members value other aspects of life. Individually fo-

Praise over punishment

When it comes to encouraging good work, praise trumps intimidation or fear every time. Parents know this; managers should too. One major company managed through intimidation and fear. In their sales group, forecasts were requested multiple times a day, and intimidation was routinely used when sales budgets were missed. Such tactics created nothing but anxiety and deprived management of the information that would help improve future sales. The good performers left as soon as possible, and the poor performers held on as long as they could survive. Create instead an environment where staff members contribute more because they want to and because they are recognized for good work they did when it occurs, not only at annual reviews.

From *Succession Transition*

The morale-building benefits of praise.

Aiden was a team leader who was known and respected for his thorough technical knowledge and his ability to produce an error-free end product. He was known for his exacting ability to find errors in the work of those he supervised, and he was just as thorough in pointing those errors out. His advisor suggested that while detecting errors was part of his role, he should also identify things his team had done well. After a month or so, his advisor asked him how it was going — did his team respond well to his compliments? Aiden offered that he'd found examples of good work but hadn't shared those observations with the team. "You only told me to look for the things they had done well. You didn't ask me to tell them!" Once he began delivering both praise and corrections, morale on his team improved, and over time he became a highly sought-out supervisor.

cused staff development has the potential to increase their psychic income — things that cannot be valued in dollars. Job satisfaction, relationship satisfaction, and a sense of security with their advisors are all things that are desired. As advisors share these methods and their advisees learn and grow, the organization will benefit as the staff development process is passed along to others. The very culture of the organization may evolve into something different as a result of the increased focus on the individual's needs.

The process of staff development begins with questions — an advisor asking an advisee questions to begin the process of reflection. This reflection begins with creating self-awareness, which we discuss in the next chapter.

APPENDIX — Chapter 1

Re-recruiting questions to ask yourself

Once you have recruited a new member to your organization or team, retaining them is important. The process of "re-recruiting" valuable staff members is an ongoing endeavor for supervisors and team leaders. Following are questions you can ask yourself on a regular basis to evaluate the strength of the staff member's commitment to your organization.

1. Do you know this staff member's number-one concern, and are you working with him/her to address it?
2. Does the team member believe their manager and leaders of the organization care?
3. Is the team member enthusiastic and passionate about the work they do?
4. Does the team member maintain a balance between personal and professional responsibilities?
5. Has the team member been asked what the organization can do to help them be more successful?

Ideally, the answers to these questions are all "Yes." Every "No" answer brings an increased risk of retention for this individual. By the way, don't assume your answers are correct. Consider asking the staff member if they agree with your assessment.

Reflection sample

Adopting a regular practice of reflecting on your career is not just enlightening — the reflection should lead to action plans that get you closer to your goals. Reflection can be done in many ways; here's a sample process.

1. Think carefully about what you want to achieve.
2. Visualize what success will look like, and write down the vision.
3. Translate your vision to a set of goals.
4. Devise a plan to reach the goals; write it down.
5. Accept that no matter what you will yourself to do, you will encounter challenges, defeats, and disappointment along the way.
6. When you run into these obstacles, remember, persistence, persistence, persistence.
7. Revisit and repeat.

"Who looks outside, dreams; who looks inside, awakes."

—Carl Jung

"Self-awareness gives you the capacity to learn from your mistakes as well as your successes. It enables you to keep growing."

—Lawrence Bossidy, corporate executive

CHAPTER TWO

Creating Self-Awareness: The importance of looking in the mirror

Here's a scenario that's repeated frequently in staff development conversations. A supervisor with the best intentions will say, "You're performing well, but there's room for improvement. You need to do more." More what? And how? As well-meaning as this advice may be, it's not precise enough to be constructive. In fact, vague feedback like this could be frustrating for the staff member who's on the receiving end.

You get the point here: An advisor who gives specific and actionable advice rather than vague observations will help their staff member jump-start the steps to improve their performance. Staff members who are clear about their strengths and the areas where they need to improve are well on the path to self-awareness. As a staff member develops a high degree of self-awareness, they'll better understand themselves and their own capabilities.

As we'll explore in this chapter, self-awareness is a powerful tool for anyone who's focused on their career development. Delivering candid feedback is just one way a conscientious advisor can help staff members improve their

Discovering your unique work DNA

The study of genetics has taught us that each individual has a unique code of DNA. The same is true of your work DNA, which encompasses your unique strengths and talents. Please consider this formula to express an equation for each individual: what you are born with (your DNA) + your set of unique experiences in life + the unique environment where you have lived (socially, politically, culturally, and historically) = your unique set of talents and strengths: your work DNA.

—*Robert Pasick*

self-awareness. They can also call out any career blind spots that may exist.

Not to be confused with self-confidence, self-awareness is recognition and knowledge of:

- Your strengths and how you can leverage them individually and to assist others.
- Your areas of improvement and how collaborating with others can balance out your shortcomings.
- Where your skills and interests stand in relationship to others and to the organization.
- Your personal preferences, which are indicators for the professional environment and the assignments that you'll find most rewarding.
- Your culture and upbringing and how they affect you personally and professionally.

When you're in a role that leverages your talents to the fullest, you compound your chances for a fulfilling career. An extrovert, for example, will be much more effective in situations that provide interpersonal opportunities, whereas an introvert may prefer to seek out assignments that can be accomplished on their own or in small groups.

The distinct personal makeup of advisors and those they supervise

When we talk about individualized staff development, the process begins with two people: an advisor and an advisee. Each is unique and has their own distinct personal makeup.

It's important for the advisor to bring their own self-awareness to the relationship and to be open (and nonjudgmental) about the unique qualities of those they supervise. Consider this:

- No one else can do exactly what you can do.
- No one else knows exactly what you know.
- No one else shares the experiences you've encountered.
- No one else sees the world the same way you see it.
- No one is better prepared to manage your future than you.

The better you understand and harness your strengths, the more successful you can become.

Dr. Robert Pasick, a corporate psychologist and lecturer at the University of Michigan Ross School of Business and the founder of Leaders Connect, explored the significance of self-awareness in his book, *Self-Aware: A Guide for Success in Work and Life.*

Dr. Pasick reminds us that:
- Self-awareness is an ongoing process.
- Self-awareness is never only about one's self only.
- No one succeeds alone.
- Self-awareness is the cornerstone of emotional intelligence.
- To learn who you are, you have to take action by trying things.

Pasick also describes the benefits of honest self-reflection for both advisors and the people they supervise. (In the Appendix, we outline a 10-step reflection process that can be used to develop self-awareness.)

The advisor's role: Self-awareness leads to career clarity

Where do we begin when we want to help staff improve their self-awareness? I like to begin by finding out where a staff person best fits in the organization. Then, once the staff member finds the right place, we can assist them in optimizing their performance in that role.

The pitfalls of being all business all the time.

One manager was struggling with interpersonal relationships with members of her team. She wasn't spending the time to connect with them, which they pointed out in upward feedback surveys. When she examined her behavior more closely, she realized that she was putting more value on getting things done than connecting with her team. (She was always "all business.") Knowing how important relationships are for staff retention, she reprioritized and committed to devoting a specific number of hours each week to spending time with her team to get to know them as people. Her interpersonal relationships and retention on her team improved. Her team even got her a card on "Boss's Day" — something that had never happened before.

Where does someone belong in an organization? It starts with understanding what's important to them and what makes them tick. Some might relish the challenges of complex problems. Others thrive when they can develop relationships with clients and fellow staff members. Some work best in teams; others work best alone. Understanding their preferences for problem-solving and team collaboration will make the best use of the advisee's skills and passions and improve their chances to excel.

For example, I've met quite a few tax people who work exceptionally well alone and consult with others only when they run into issues where they need help. At the other end of the spectrum are the staff members who enjoy teamwork and feed off the dynamic energy of collaborating with others. If your organization has various roles that staff can explore, exposing them to these options early in their careers can be the first step for successful staff development. The opportunity to experience multiple departments, practice areas, or functions in an organization provides a rich learning opportunity as well as experiences that may help your staff members pinpoint exactly what inspires them.

At Plante Moran, new hires in audit and tax are given a couple of years to determine which specific service area and/or industry they will focus on for their career. This allows them to learn the core requirements of their position while spending time in a variety of engagements. The intention is to hire good people first, even if finding out exactly where they fit takes a little time. Occasionally, we'll discover an individual who doesn't have the proper skill set, can't overcome their blind spots, or may just be the wrong fit for the organization. When that happens, it requires additional attention and potentially involvement of a colleague to address the situation. No doubt you've had the same experience and have worked with your HR team to find the right solution.

An advisor who's guiding an individual at a critical juncture early in their career can focus on a few basic concepts. What aspects of their work does the advisee like, and which discipline appeals to them the most? What do they prefer about the style, the environment, or the complexity of their projects? The following questions are good conversation starters, and remember, the goal is to get the advisee thinking about their preferences.

- What have you done recently that you really enjoyed?
- What are you attracted to?
- What type of work environment do you like?
- What kinds of clients do you like working with?
- Who do you like working with and why?
- What's been your best experience in the last few months?
- What are the constants in the things you liked that attracted you?

• What jobs have you performed well on recently?

• What jobs have been a challenge for you recently?

The advisor's role is to lead the advisee on the path of self-discovery, and the process may be more of an art than a science. But don't overcomplicate it. Sometimes you get insights after just three to five questions. By listening to the advisee's answers, the advisor will get a notion for what follow-up questions to ask. It's also worth noting that these questions don't need to be limited to a formal setting. In fact, an informal conversation may get more honest responses from a staff member who's relaxed and not worried about giving the correct answer.

It's important for the advisee to realize that their advisors have their best interests in mind and want them to find where they fit best and help get them to that place within the organization. Once they've been through this experience, hopefully it's something they'll be able to use to advise staff they'll supervise in the future.

Career clarity after finding her true strength.

Annabella had been an audit manager for 11 years and was serving clients well. She wanted to take the next step to partner, but her career path was cloudy. She'd been told that she was "on track" to make partner, but it wasn't clear what she needed to do next. As a client server, she excelled in delivering audits, but the duties required to develop and grow her own practice were murky, and achieving in this area would be essential if she were to become an audit partner. After several one-on-one sessions with an advisor to ask probing questions about her true preferences, one thing stood out: Her passion was solving problems by understanding the technical requirements of an audit and financial statement presentations. In the end, she realized that she'd be most effective as a technical resource serving on the professional standards team rather than as an audit partner. Once she uncovered her true strength and found out where she really belonged, she flourished and ultimately became a partner.

Once we determine where we think the advisee sees themselves in the organization, we can support them in moving in that direction. Some staff members may need additional time and exposure to multiple roles, which could mean a lengthy process. As time passes, the advisee should be getting closer to where they belong. With each step forward, they'll be happier and more productive, which is a benefit to the individual and the organization.

Using a Gap Analysis

When it looks like the staff member is settled in where they belong, it's time to consider other tools that can clarify where they stand. Many organizations use a 360-degree analysis to gather feedback on a staff member from their colleagues, which could be people they supervise, their peers, and those who supervise them. Studies estimate that 60% of U.S. companies use some form of 360-degree analysis to measure performance.

Another method that will enhance a staff member's self-awareness is a Gap Analysis, a tool that's quick, easy-to-use, and delivers a very clear analysis of strengths to leverage and areas to improve. Simply put, a Gap Analysis determines how well a staff member is performing by using criteria that are clear and understood by both the advisor and the advisee. A Gap Analysis is effective because it unveils tangible opportunities for improvement (wide gaps), which means the advisor can steer clear of vague recommendations such as "working harder" or "improving" or "doing more." It also highlights areas of strength (small to no gaps), which staff members should continue to foster as they progress in their careers.

8 Point Gap Analysis—

Independent Appraisal by Individual, Advisory Team, Team Partner, or Other Partner(s)

- Client Focus/Relationship Management
- Communications
- Leadership/Management
- Staff Relations
- Staff Development
- Technical Skills
- Problem Solving
- Network/Practice Development

The starting point for the Gap Analysis demonstrated here is Plante Moran's key competencies. These competencies are a set of behaviors the firm considers necessary for individual progress no matter the staff member's role. The concepts have evolved over time and are fundamental to managing performance. Your organization may have its own unique competencies, but if you don't, feel free to use these eight as a starting point for a Gap Analysis (see the Appendix for definitions):

1. Client Focus/Relationship Management
2. Communications
3. Leadership/Management
4. Staff Relations
5. Staff Development
6. Technical Skills
7. Problem Solving
8. Network/Practice Development

(You may be wondering, why are Staff Relations and Staff Development separate competencies? It's because they're different — and they're both critical and important to attracting and retaining staff for the long term.) When a staff member shows strong ability in these competencies, it's an indication they'll be able to grow and build their own teams as they progress in their careers.

So how does the Gap Analysis work? The first step is for the advisee to rate themselves on a scale of 1 to 10 for each competency. They perform this analysis twice, once comparing themselves to their peers and once comparing themselves to those in the role they'd progress into next (the next step on their career path).

We then ask two or three of the advisee's supervisors to provide the same ratings, comparing the advisee to their peers and their supervisors. None of the results are shared until all of the individual appraisals are complete. While this might sound like a lot of work, it usually takes no more than five to 10 minutes per analysis. It's not intended for the person to spend a lot of time doing self-analysis. In fact, it works best with swift analysis. We then gather the results and compare their self-analysis with the analysis provided by the supervisors to see what we can learn.

The advisee may have given themselves a "6" on Communication, while the supervisors may have given them a "4." They may have rated themselves as an "8" on Technical Skills and received

The value of candor

A popular saying is "candor is kindness." Telling someone the truth can be challenging, but failing to communicate a crucial truth only hurts the person who most needs to hear it. These corrections can make a difference in a person's career, learning, and overall comfort level.

the same rating from their supervisors. The former calls for attention, while the latter does not. Whenever there's a difference of opinion with a gap of two or more points on one of the eight categories, it usually indicates an area where the advisee needs improvement. The gap shows a staff member is unaware of an area where they may be deficient (a blind spot), and this would lead to a discussion about specific ways to improve in that category. In addition, the Gap Analysis may highlight an absolutely low rating, which will also require attention.

An advisee who wants to level up and be promoted can learn a lot from the ratings that compare their current ability to what's expected for a performer in the next tier or role. If there are wide gaps to fill from their current behavior to what's expected at the next level, the advisee can create an action plan to address those gaps.

Sometimes, an advisee underrates their performance. This may be a self-awareness issue or possibly because the advisee overestimates the requirements of the job. These, too, can be learning moments for an advisee.

The Gap Analysis shows us what to focus on with specificity. Such an analysis allows us to quantify and label the advisee's strengths and weaknesses and establishes a consistent grading scale. This avoids the vagueness of telling someone they have room for improvement. Improve? Yes, here is where specific improvement is needed. The more specific the advice is the better: For example, saying "you need to improve in communication" is obviously better than "you need to improve," but "you need to work on coming across as more personable and warm" is even better.

Throughout this process, candor is both necessary and valuable because, as the saying goes, "candor is kindness." An advisor must be willing to be honest about addressing areas for improvement revealed by the Gap Analysis. An advisee who's willing to listen and learn will be able to grow in the areas that are identified. The advisor can further assist by identifying specific and defined action steps that would close the gap. The advisee ideally should be held accountable for working on these tasks.

It's important for the advisor to create realistic expectations for improvement. A very serious gap might take time to close. As long as the advisee is making meaningful and steady improvement, it may be acceptable. It's important for advisees to understand that this process is designed to move them along a path for improvement and the gaps aren't viewed as negatives in the traditional sense. In other words, we'll make an evaluation about what needs to improve and what will lead to improvement. The advisor must be sure the advisee understands this and knows where to turn for help.

Over the years, I've worked with staff at various levels and have seen them flourish, even though they had competencies that needed work. A person who needs development in an area or two isn't deficient by any means, especially if they're working on improvement. They may stand for promotion so long as they're making progress.

While we've focused on the deficiencies revealed by a Gap Analysis, that's not to devalue the strengths that will come to light. Some might say that it's better to focus on what you're good at rather than to get stuck only focusing on your areas for development. Someone with noteworthy strengths should be encouraged to nurture and optimize them. In some cases, we've seen strong evidence of a particular ability/talent leading a staff member in an entirely different direction. After a Gap Analysis, the advisee will be more aware of their strengths, and, working closely with their advisor, they'll look for ways to use them to their best advantage.

The Gap Analysis is a tool best used starting with staff that have four to six years of experience — often around the time someone becomes a beginning manager — and then repeated every couple of years thereafter. That said, I've also done these Gap Analyses with Plante Moran partners. Experience shows most partners have at

Specific feedback for better staff development.
Following a Gap Analysis, Barbara recognized that improving her staff development skills would help her to build a stronger team. The skill she wanted to work on was giving direct feedback. "If you don't give people direct feedback, you're hurting them in the long term," she recalled. She implemented a plan by which every team member would provide instant feedback to each other after a client meeting. They'd ask, "How did you think the meeting went? What did you do well? What could we have done differently? How did I do? How did you do?" According to Barbara, the team she started with continues to do the round-robin direct feedback to this day. "It works because it's on the spot, it's constructive, and people are open to it," she explains. The team has grown tremendously, and the process is now so ingrained that one person comes out of meetings and gives himself self-feedback.

least two strong characteristics, sometimes three. They may meet expectations on a few items, and then they usually have one or two areas for improvement. This is not uncommon — even for the most experienced partners. It's a career-long, continuous improvement process, but it's good for advisors and advisees to recognize that no one is perfect, not even them.

Once the advisor has worked to elevate the advisee's self-awareness, the next area of focus is helping them achieve their balance.

Hurdle Rate - To Become a Partner - What Is Your Differentiator?

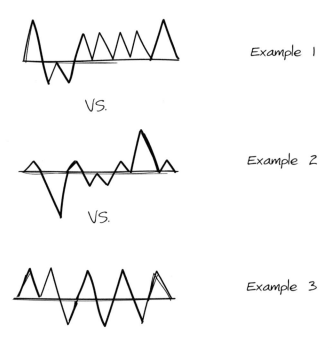

VS.

VS.

Example 1

Example 2

Example 3

This illustration demonstrates that partners in a firm aren't perfect and may need to focus on competency areas even after they have become partners. The baseline indicates expected performance on the eight behaviors that we evaluate in a Gap Analysis. Example 1 represents a "typical" partner profile: a couple of outstanding strengths and several that are above or below the expected level. The areas below the line will be competencies they'll continue to focus on for the rest of their career. Example 2 is an unusual example and depicts someone who may have one tremendous area of strength and one area that will require significant focus in the future. An individual with this profile would need special attention to leverage the strength and minimize the impact of the deficiency. Example 3 identifies someone who is average overall; they don't stand out. An individual with this profile may not become a partner. They're a fine performer but they haven't adequately developed their competencies and may be better suited for some other role.

APPENDIX — Chapter 2

Developing Self-Awareness — A 10-step process

1. Learn to know and to appreciate your strengths.
2. Focus on what really interests you and about what you are passionate.
3. Find people who can give you honest feedback about who you are and how you are perceived by others.
4. Take self-assessments to better understand your personality style and motivations.
5. Recognize different ways that you're thinking and the beliefs that can impose self-limitations on you.
6. Learn how you fit into the path blazed by your ancestors and family. Realize your story is a continuation of theirs.
7. Discover how the culture you grew up in and live in now affects how you are as a person.
8. Realize that to become truly self-aware you must take risks and be willing to learn from them.
9. Reflect on the big questions:
   • Why are you here on earth?
   • What is your purpose in life?
   • In what ways is it important for you to make a difference?
10. Reflect on what "well-being" means for you: What is the right balance between career, social well-being, financial success, and physical and mental well-being?

Gap Analysis competencies

The following are standard definitions of competencies that may be evaluated in a Gap Analysis. These competency definitions could be included as part of your organization's performance management system.

Client Focus/Relationship Management

Focuses on developing effective client relationships and providing high-quality, professional service to clients (internal and/or external) that results in a knowledge and understanding of their needs and service that exceeds expectations.

Communications

Explains or conveys information to others through presentation, conversation, or written communication to gain support or cause others to take action; presents information to others in a proactive or responsive manner and utilizes routine communication to build relationships.

Leadership/Management

Leads/energizes others to pursue excellence and utilize their skills, while making significant contributions (on behalf of the client or firm); effectively utilizes and leverages skills, experience, and resources to manage task, project, or practice.

Staff Relations

Builds and maintains positive relationships to achieve objectives. Practices "Golden Rule" in all relationships.

Staff Development

Commits to develop and expand their abilities to improve performance and contributes to the development of others.

Technical Skills

Develops, understands, and applies specialized knowledge through experience, interaction with others, and formal training for the overall benefit of the firm; effectively utilizes appropriate technology to increase productivity and improve client service (internal and external).

Problem Solving

Uses sound judgment and resourceful/analytical perspective to create viable solutions for clients (internal and/or external) that are consistent with firm values and Service Group/ Practice vision.

Network/Practice Development

Contributes directly and indirectly to maintaining and growing the business.

"Never get so busy making a living that you forget to make a life."

—Dolly Parton

— ✶ —

"Attaining balance is a lifetime workout, and even for the well-balanced person, balance is a wobbling back and forth on the tightrope."

—Bob Petz, former HR director, Plante Moran

— ✶ —

"You can't do a good job if your job is all you do."

—Anonymous

CHAPTER THREE

Balance: Techniques to integrate all aspects of "life"

All of us have seen this caricature about the stereotypical demands of corporate culture: Picture a harried and overworked manager who's trying hard to please an overbearing boss. The manager's co-workers, who are equally overworked and frustrated, pay the price also. Their family lives may suffer because there's no time for the personal activities they'd like to pursue. In a work environment like this, everyone is at risk for leaving. But it doesn't have to be that way.

From boss to manager to staff, this caricature illustrates what happens when personal imbalance cascades in today's work world. The work environment suffers when staff members are stressed, out of sorts, easily distracted, and constantly struggling to achieve their potential. In contrast, a staff person whose life is considerably in balance makes a meaningful contribution at home, in their organization, and in the community. The whole person comes to work.

In most professional settings, gone are the days when work is done entirely in the office. Thanks to technology, many people may work remotely, some or all of the time, and during off-hours. People can read emails while waiting with an elderly parent at the doctor's office, and they can fire up their laptops to do work after the kids are in bed. Work-around-the clock is possible, but it shouldn't mean that work never ends. Staff members want to have — and deserve to have — balanced lives. Advisors who recognize the stresses their staff face and pro-actively help them balance competing interests at work and beyond the office will improve the environment for all with increased productivity, better staff retention, and an improved culture. The ideal situation is when advisors model balanced behavior in their own lives and serve as an example for their team members.

Consider life's "spheres of influence"

Work-life balance may be something of a misnomer. It's important to realize that no one can expect a life in perfect balance all the time; your life may not be balanced each and every day. It's more realistic to strive for overall balance that takes into account the ebb and flow of personal, family, professional, and community factors that will impact our lives at a given time. For example, someone may work extraordinary hours during a new product launch, an unavoidable fact of life. At other times, a 40-hour workweek may be the norm.

Another way to think about balance is to consider life as three fluid spheres of influence: work, personal, and community. (Yes, community. Most of us want to have an impact, and not just at

Spheres of Influence

work, so let's remember that community activities are part of the balance mix.) These spheres affect our life balance because they make demands on our time, energy, and attention. Understand that these spheres aren't static: They grow and shrink in relation to each other. Life events such as a marriage, birth, or death will cause our personal sphere to expand. A peak busy season assignment may require more emphasis on work-related matters. When you're involved with a major event for a community organization, the project may demand extreme attention during that time. If one of the spheres of influence remains too large for too long, our balance is impacted. We may need to ride it out and adjust elsewhere, or re-evaluate and possibly reduce our commitment.

Covering all the bases, at work, home, and in the community.

Brendan was an extremely talented senior manager. With a wife and three children, he felt constrained. "I'm always behind, and I haven't been able to use my paid time off," he complained. Through several conversations with an advisor, he developed techniques to create collaboration, learned to delegate, and figured out where he could focus his time. He also evaluated his work, personal, and community commitments to better understand the flow of his calendar. Knowing that there would be "seasons" of heavy work commitments, Brendan paid a lot of attention to "building emotional bank accounts" by making deposits with his clients, wife, and co-workers. With his wife, the emotional bank accounts included making time for date nights on a regular basis and bringing home flowers "just because." Knowing that you have maintained a positive balance in your emotional bank account can give you comfort for the occasional "misstep."

Balance is also individual, and to achieve it, each person must figure out what it takes for them — the individual. It might even change over time. It's also worth noting that balance applies to everyone, whatever their circumstances may be. Work, family, hobbies, and community involvement may vary depending on the phase of the career. This isn't an exact science. Find the sweet spot — what's important — and work toward that.

Balance: A simple place to start

An advisor can expect the balance question to come up early in the relationship with their staff members — it's just that important. When that happens, one approach is to help the individual zero in on their personal "ecosystem" and encourage them to explore how these influences affect their overall balance. This exercise encourages an individual to focus on what's important to them, versus what they think is expected of them. The staff member is asked to imagine themselves at the center of a diagram, orbited by five spheres that represent the main factors affecting their life — typically health, family, work, social life, and civic/community activity. All are significant, but many people let some of them slip by the wayside when another element dominates.

Personal Ecosystem

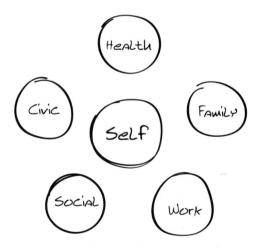

The individual draws a line from the Self to each sphere. If the relationship is strong with no major issues, the line is solid. If the relationship is strained in some way, or there's unfinished business or minor problems, the line is dotted. If the relationship has a serious problem, the line is jagged.

A person who does this exercise honestly can quickly pinpoint areas where there's tension, stress, or some other issue interfering with that aspect of their life. They may also be able to anticipate issues that arise because of seasonal activities. For example, a professional with seasonal or project duties will know which parts of the year will be busy due to the nature of their assignments. Most specialties have ebbs and flows that can be anticipated and planned for in advance.

The next step is to help the staff member diagnose the "root cause" of the issue. This is where the life experiences of the advisor may play a major role. If an advisee "doesn't have enough time" to finish tasks, what's causing the time shortage? Are they saying "Yes" to every request they receive to help on a project? Are they overcommitted? Could they regain some of their time by delegating tasks to others? Would hiring someone to help with housework free up their time? Sometimes, it takes the perspective of another person, especially one with experience, to spot what might be causing a colleague to be spreading themselves too thin.

Take charge of your calendar and learn to say "No."

For Chloe, the transition from a chaotic calendar to life in balance took 18 months. At the beginning, she never said "No" to any request, and her schedule was driven by whoever was making the most noise. She had no external network because she was so busy, and she didn't have an internal network, either. Finally, she had yet to develop delegation skills, deciding just to take everything on her own shoulders. With the help of her advisor, she figured out how many hours she wanted to work. Next, she scheduled her vacation — and took it. When she came back, refreshed, she became more intentional about her time. She added her child's activities to her calendar and protected the time. She factored in her awareness about achieving balance overall, not just day to day. And, on the counsel of her advisor, she said "No" four times every week, just to get comfortable with the idea. Finally, she laid out a two-year plan for what she wanted to be known for and stuck to it.

Much of the literature on time management recommends adopting a discipline of setting aside time to schedule personal and professional priorities. For most people, this can be achieved with a weekly check-in where you inventory long- and short-term projects and map out the goals and priorities for the week ahead. This would include any deadlines, meetings, family appointments, and personal goals. My recommendation is to set aside 30–60 minutes at the same time each week for a personal "balance check" to evaluate where you may be out of balance or which areas of your life need attention. The time spent on this weekly check-in can move us closer to the overall life balance that we strive to achieve.

This is also a time when the advisor can lead by example. One technique is to make it a practice to include your personal commitments on shared work calendars, whether it's a child's sport activity, a manicure, or a parent's doctor's appointment. This leads to transparency among the team and overtly acknowledges that the advisor has a life and it's OK for their staff to have one, too.

Finding your "Personal Sweet Spot"

For most people, finding balance can be a career-long journey. An advisor who wants to give their staff members a jump-start on that path can encourage an exercise called finding the "Personal Sweet Spot." This exercise focuses on four key attributes that will maximize their balance and personal satisfaction. The goal is to achieve a level of satisfaction in the following areas:

1. Passion about your work
2. Utilization of your unique combination of talents
3. Meeting the financial needs of you and your family
4. Emotional, ethical, and societal values you hold dear

The intersection of the four attributes represents the individual's Personal Sweet Spot.

The Sweet Spot exercise is something that an advisee is encouraged to do on their own when they have quiet time to reflect. It's designed to highlight the professional and personal areas that are most important to them and where their lives will be properly balanced and personally rewarding. Completing this exercise also requires self-awareness because it gets to the heart of their personal and professional preferences, talents, and values. (See the Appendix for additional questions to consider for the Sweet Spot

Personal Sweet Spot

Passion

1. What activity brings you the most joy in your life?

_____

_____

2. What do you love to do so much that you would do it even if you weren't being paid for it?

_____

_____

Unique Talents

1. What do you do better than most everybody you know?

_____

_____

2. What are you succeeding at now or you have been succeeding at since you were a teenager?

_____

_____

3. What are you not good at?

_____

Are you Passionate about it?

Are you using your talents to the fullest?

Can you get paid enough?

Does the community value what you do?

Financial

1. How much money do you need to be paid to sustain your desired lifestyle?

_____

_____

_____

_____

Values

1. Describe an organization that would enable you to uphold your ethics and societal values while simultaneously enabling you to maintain your desired work-family balance.

_____

_____

_____

_____

exercise. This should be a personal exercise that the advisee can decide to share, or not, depending on their preference.)

In all the years I've met with staff to introduce this exercise, no two advisees have ever been the same with respect to where they found themselves. A typical example might be the staff member who is working hard and doing well. They meet their soulmate and decide to settle down, buy a house, and start a family. If they get a job offer that pays substantially more, they'll be tempted to take the offer and jump for the money. After all, isn't that the "right" thing to do at this point? Not necessarily, as it might throw off their balance. Leaving a place where they'd achieved their "sweet spot" in exchange for a larger salary might be a long-term mistake. What if the new place is boring or a grind? The key is to ask: What's important to you, and what's the long-term impact?

Let's look at an example. Caleb, a Plante Moran partner, left the firm after receiving an offer that substantially increased his compensation. After a couple of years, he came back. "I didn't know how important the people here were to me. What I was doing and the challenges and variety of work I dealt with here were also important to me. I made a lot of money, but I wasn't happy." People may go for the money because it's so attractive. But is it worth giving up their life balance to do so?

Much of staff development is helping advisees understand what their work balance needs to be to keep them satisfied and engaged. Some of the "re-recruiting" questions provided in the Appendix to

Learning the importance of "me time."
Delia recalls an advisor who gave concrete guidance on maintaining balance. "He reminded me to plan ahead and schedule my vacations and days off to keep my sanity. He recommended that I be intentional about my non-billable time so that I made room for practice development, recruiting, trainings, and other things that often get left behind. He also said to find time for "me," take care of myself, and do the things that I like to do for fun. By putting myself last and meeting everyone else's needs first, that was a surefire way to burn myself out."

Chapter 1 are useful points of conversation that will help advisors understand where their staff members are on the work-balance tightrope. While the Sweet Spot is something to strive for, it might not be easily obtainable. It takes time and honest reflection: There's nothing simple about finding your Sweet Spot destination.

People need to understand that their Sweet Spot will evolve over time, and life events such as a divorce, a death in the family, or illness will have an impact. A younger professional, recently married, may have very different aspirations than they'll have a decade or two later. This is perfectly normal and merely something to consider along the way.

As elusive as balance may be, it's something that we want for ourselves and for others. Consistent attention to achieving balance is time well spent and is a key element to creating satisfaction in all aspects of life. As an advisor, you may want to challenge the advisee to see if they're emphasizing the right "life" categories. Staying attuned to their team members and using these exercises helps an advisor spot potential issues before there's a crisis. Not only does that benefit the staff member, but it also models the type of behavior that will be useful to them in their careers.

APPENDIX — Chapter 3

Key traits of balanced leaders
Balance isn't just a challenge for new staff — it's also a challenge for seasoned team leaders. Balance has even more impact for leaders because it has a trickle-down effect on the team being led. Here are 20 principles that can define a balanced leader:

1. You balance your needs with those of others in your family.
2. You balance your needs with those of others in your organization.
3. You manage your energy.
4. You manage your time.
5. You adhere to your values.
6. You keep an optimistic outlook while remaining realistic.
7. You cultivate consistency while adapting to change.
8. You practice self-reflection.
9. You maintain your emotional composure.
10. You recognize and manage your blind spots.

11. You leverage your strengths while managing your weaknesses.
12. You try to see yourself as others see you.
13. You alternate periods of hard work with periods of sustained rest.
14. You play as hard as you work.
15. You take chances and make mistakes.
16. You acknowledge your mistakes.
17. You learn from your mistakes.
18. You maintain a good sense of humor.
19. You cultivate friends and relatives to keep you on the right path.
20. You never do any of this alone.

This list is intended to get you thinking about what may impact your balance and which areas may be included when you develop your own action plan to get back in balance.

Guiding questions to find your "Sweet Spot"

When you're doing the "Sweet Spot" exercise, answering these questions will help you focus in on the specific attributes you value. Determining your level of satisfaction within each attribute will require self-reflection and challenging the status quo as it exists today.

Passion

1. What do you seek to learn more about through reading, television, conversations, etc.?
2. Which newspapers, magazines, or websites do you subscribe to, and which section do you read first?
3. Where do you contribute your time and money?
4. What interests do you have now that you also had before the age of 18?
5. What cause or topic makes you feel "fire in your belly"?
6. If you won the lottery, what activities would you continue to do even if you didn't need to do them for the money?
7. On the days when you're excited about going to work, what is it you're looking forward to doing?

Value

1. What do you care deeply about? For example: What do you read about? Talk about? Think about?
2. Notice what brings you the most joy in life. This is a key clue to understanding your passion.
3. Ask yourself, "When I have had a great day, what was I doing and what was I not doing?"
4. What topic(s) most evoke(s) a strong emotional reaction? Passion is emotion.
5. If you ask other people, what do they say you are passionate about? You might consider sending an email to people who know you well to ask them how they see you.

Unique talents

1. What activities seem natural and somewhat automatic to you?
2. What roles do others generally ask you to fulfill?
3. What tasks do you generally try to avoid?
4. What circumstances generally lead to a successful result?
5. What roles do you like to volunteer for?

Financial

1. Explore how much money is enough for you.
2. Make a hard analysis about how much of a risk-taker you are about money and how anxious you get when there's no secure path for making money every month. Entrepreneurial activities aren't for those who are uncomfortable with risk-taking and require a steady paycheck.
3. These days, people are also willing to pay for exceptional experiences. Creative types need to think about how they can create a great experience that will be valued in the marketplace.
4. Look beyond money to the important resources of time and energy. For some people, having adequate time is more important than having a lot of money.

To get the most out of this process, we recommend that you adopt a "Reflection Cycle" that includes taking your "Sweet Spot" conclusions, envisioning what success looks like to achieve them, writing down specific goals, creating and acting on your plan to achieve those goals (don't forget that you will encounter challenges and disappointments), and, finally, monitoring and reflecting on your progress. See Appendix Chapter 1 for more on the Reflection Cycle.

Questions to ask when considering a career change

A staff member may request input from an advisor when they are considering a career change. When this happens, the advisor should put aside their biases, listen, and truly try to consider what is in the staff member's best interest. The following exercise will help an advisee to evaluate whether a change in career is appropriate or not.

1. Make a list of risks on both sides of the ledger: the risks of entering a new career path vs. the risks of staying in the current role.

2. Repeat step 1 with the current role (flip the focus).

3. Do the "Sweet Spot" exercise, where you assess the intersection between your passions, your unique combination of skills and talents, your values, and your financial needs and goals.

4. Determine how close you are to your "Sweet Spot" in your current role and how close you would be in the alternate role or career being considered.

5. Assess your history of risk-taking. Ask what the consequences have been of failing to take a risk.

6. Ask yourself what the worst thing that could happen would be if you took the risk. Second, ask yourself, "If the worst thing happened, would I be able to handle it?"

7. Consider this adage: "The most dangerous place in the world is our comfort zone." Do you agree?

"Staff development isn't something we hand you. The staff person needs to have the desire and ability to take the feedback and make actionable changes."

—Plante Moran partner

"Tell me and I forget. Teach me and I may remember. Involve me and I learn."

—Old proverb

CHAPTER FOUR

Staff Development: The impact of one-size-fits-one supervision

Two days after I made partner, I went on a client call with a senior partner at the firm. As you can imagine, I had the enthusiasm and self-confidence of a new partner and was feeling pretty good about my achievement. While I was in the car returning from the meeting, the senior partner asked me how I thought the meeting went. I replied that it went very well, but suggested the client had difficulty hearing him because he tended to talk with his chin in his hand and some of his comments were muffled. He was gracious and thanked me for that observation. I then asked him how he thought the meeting went, and he offered six observations about things that I did well and areas that could be improved. Those six things I remember to this day; they included letting people finish their sentences and not assuming that you know what someone is going to say. I might add my own key takeaway: Make sure your brain is on before engaging mouth and offering observations!

That episode is a mini-playbook for effective staff development: The observations were delivered in the context of a trusting and open relationship; the

"When you look at where people should be in management, it varies according to their personality, disposition, skills, and a host of other personal factors. Some folks excel in clearly defined situations while others prosper when the circumstances are vague and they have to figure things out. Some people thrive when their innovative skills are tapped. You just take a look at the spectrum of people and skills, find the highest and best use, put those people in those spots, and let them go."

From *Succession Transition*

feedback was candid and specific to the individual in their circumstance; it was delivered in the moment, just at the time when I was best able to receive it. The fact that 35 years later I can still recall the feedback from that day is a testament to the value of the message and the effectiveness of the person delivering the advice. We could all be fortunate to be able to develop staff in that manner.

Formal performance appraisals have a place, but real-time feedback works, too.
"There's nothing more effective than delivering feedback in the moment," says Dylan, who compares it to the real-time learning he experienced when a golf coach videotaped his golf swing. An advisee will learn more from real-time feedback. "Your comments can be positive or negative, but what's important is addressing them on the spot. Then there's no time to revise history."

Helping staff grow and develop can be one of the most rewarding parts of your career. Whether your role is that of a coach, mentor, advisory team member, or team partner, your staff development skills will grow and evolve based on your own experience. Your goal is to groom future generations by providing meaningful feedback, presenting them with options that will promote their growth, leverage their development, and create clarity for their future. That includes being aware of their shortcomings or gaps, as discussed in Chapter 2, and creating opportunities to bridge those gaps. As long as you remember that no two individuals are the same and that they learn at different rates, you'll be remembered as a helpful and effective advisor who helped your staff members grow and progress in their careers. Their success and contributions to the organization will be part of your future legacy.

Basics for individually focused staff development

Most of us can remember the early stages of our careers when the performance criteria and our career path were vague. More than anything, we wanted information from an informed source because our

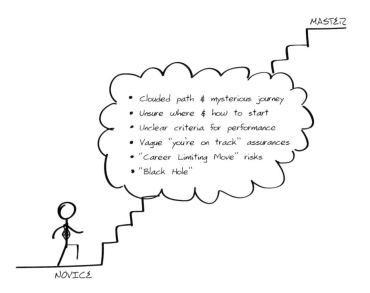

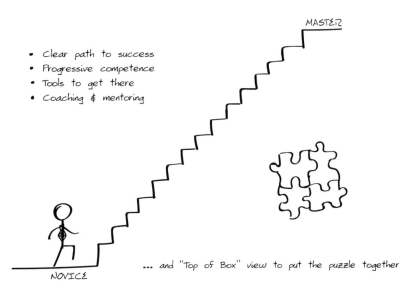

notions about career development were tinged with uncertainty and mixed messages from peers and advisors. An advisor who is prepared to help can clear the cloudiness and define the path their advisees should follow, no matter which stage of their career they are in.

Most advisors will have routine check-in meetings with those on their team as well as formal performance management or career planning meetings. The formal meetings are usually dedicated to evaluating progress over a specific time period and to set goals for the future. I've found that the best way to allocate time in these meetings is the 80-20 rule: 80% of the time looking ahead and 20% of the time looking back. The Appendix to this chapter includes a variety of conversation starters, meeting tips, guidelines for establishing action plans, and advice for difficult conversations. In this chapter, we'll focus on additional ways that advisors can support their staff's development by addressing their individual and specific needs.

Ellen recalls tough, but necessary, feedback that was delivered in the moment.

"When I'd been at the firm for five years, the lead partner and I had to deliver a serious message to a client about a major audit finding — a fraud situation. As you can imagine, this was an intense and very grave meeting where our message to the client was, 'You must disclose these findings to the regulators.' After the meeting, the partner said, 'Let's talk about the meeting,' so we stopped at a coffee shop. He told me, 'I know you don't do it on purpose, but this was a serious meeting, and you have a nervous laugh.' That was the first time someone gave me personal feedback about the nonverbal communication that I conveyed. It was important for me to hear that so I could address it in future situations. This was nontechnical education that was important to receive."

When we think about individualized staff development, there are a number of tools that advisors have at their disposal.

One helpful tool is the Pyramid of Progress, which outlines the interpersonal phases of learning and development from the

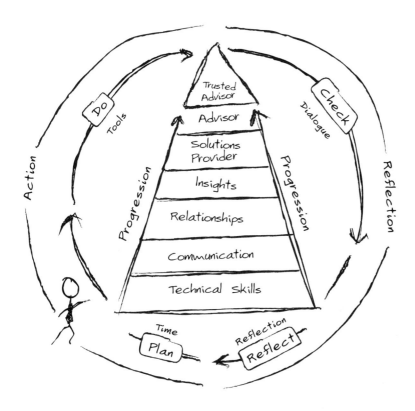

The Pyramid of Progress
A Plante Moran Relationship Development Model

early days of a career to the ultimate state as a trusted advisor to both clients and fellow staff members. It's a straightforward way to visualize the phases for an advisee and show how they build on one another. A key point to remember is that the Pyramid isn't just about developing the technical skills required for a given position. For example, it's not only about an architect learning better design skills or a consultant getting a better grasp of detailed project requirements.

The base of the pyramid is "Technical Skills," which captures our primary responsibility to our clients and each other: to be at the top of the game in our technical knowledge, which, no contest, is the fundamental reason clients hire us. A new hire (let's call her Amy) is expected to have the basic skills ("book learning") for her role, but formal training programs and on-the-job work experiences will build these skills. As these experiences compound, ideally technical capabilities will grow, helping her gain the attention and respect of clients and colleagues.

Communication skills, the next building block on the pyramid, will develop as Amy translates her technical knowledge and learns to communicate effectively with others. She understands communication protocols — when to raise questions and how to handle issues that come up. When peers and clients come to Amy with questions or problems, she addresses their issues openly and forthrightly.

Effective interpersonal relationships are the next stop on the pyramid. Amy is now technically adept and communicates well, and she'll also learn to reach out to others and develop good relationships. Now someone with a problem can call on her because she's given good advice in the past. In answering, Amy imparts insight.

Insight then puts Amy in a position where her colleagues think, "Whenever I talk to her, I get an insight and options to consider, so I'm going to come to her whenever I have a problem." The problem may not even have anything to do with work. As Amy helps others, she evolves into a reliable problem-solver.

Problems-solvers can offer solutions in a variety of ways, and Amy will draw upon her technical knowledge, experiences, and other relationships. The bottom line is other staff members and clients come to her before they call anyone else. She has become an advisor and, over time, can grow and become a trusted advisor.

As a trusted advisor to others, Amy will be there no matter the topic. She can be counted on to help in any number of ways. Since Amy is a trusted advisor to a client, it wouldn't be unusual for the client to seek her input about matters related to their family and other nonbusiness matters. The depth of the relationship is such that Amy and her clients value each other's time and expertise. She may not be the trusted advisor to every client she helps, but ideally someone at the organization should be.

Additionally, each level in the Pyramid of Progress includes the "Plan, Do, Check, and Reflect" cycle. Any given task or assignment begins with a plan. This might be a project, a recurring assignment, or a topic of research. The staff member executes the plan — the "do" — and performs the task. Then they check the outcome. Reflection on that outcome will lend them insight into how performance can

Making the leap from insight to advisor.
Frances helped one manager expand his skills beyond technical expertise to advisor. "The best developers don't just point out what's wrong; they help you fix it through experiential learning," she said. One talented manager was outstanding in every way. He was a great auditor, his jobs were on budget, and there were never problems, but one of his impediments to becoming a partner wasn't being consultative enough. When asked how he could stretch beyond his compliance-based work, the manager said there was no time for that. Frances gave him a goal: In the next year, he should work on a designated number of assignments that had nothing to do with audit/taxes. "As luck would have it, the manager had one client who called all the time. He was able to build his advisory skills in a safe environment with a client where he had a level of comfort." Gaining experience responding to the client's questions was exactly what this manager needed to become comfortable and effective as an advisor.

be elevated on future tasks or provide a sense of satisfaction or a moment to bask in the knowledge of a job well done.

Growing skills by collaborating with others

Most of us can recall an experience when the dynamic synergy of working with someone else on an assignment expanded our understanding and problem solving exponentially. When an advisor finds a beneficial opportunity to pair up staff members on projects, the results can produce untold benefits for each of them, the organization, and especially the client. These creative pairings can connect people at different experience levels, from different disciplines, or even different personality types. Ideally, both staff members will grow from the relationship.

One thing to remember when pairing staff members on projects is pacer theory. According to pacer theory, when someone wants to learn from a person more skilled than they are, it doesn't help if they're matched with a person who's significantly more advanced.

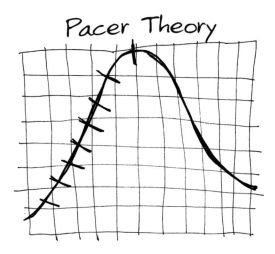

Pacer Theory

The idea is to move at a pace within their comfort zone while also being stretched. A beginner wouldn't build their tennis skills by playing against Serena or Venus Williams — they simply couldn't keep up with things like skill, speed, technique, or execution. Rather, find a partner who's better but not too far out of reach from the skill level of the learner.

It's also beneficial to pair staff members from different disciplines or other focus areas. Teaming up with a colleague with a different perspective can foster stronger problem-solving approaches, more insights, and better results. An advisor can encourage their staff members to build a diverse internal network with those who have different skills; it can be an asset for staff members who want to improve their own performance and help the organization and its clients.

Collaboration among staff members has other benefits that might not seem apparent at first glance. At one point, Plante Moran wanted to encourage collaboration on new business pursuits and decided to test a program where partners who tried to be lone rangers weren't rewarded for bringing in new clients on their own. When two or more individuals were involved in landing a client, all were rewarded. The firm learned that when multiple people were active in a pursuit, the close rate improved and ultimately led to better client retention. Staff members also noticed improvements in the pursuit process: It was much easier to keep presentations on track and make sure nothing potentially important to the client prospect was missed. Questions raised by the potential client were easier to answer, and the clients were pleased with the expertise and attention they received. Likewise, the clients who had been brought aboard by a pursuit team versus an individual were less likely to leave the firm when one staff member was no longer involved. They might miss the one person who moved on, but the others who were there in the beginning were still around to serve them and minimized the impact of the change.

The value of experiential learning

Most organizations offer formal training programs that teach staff the hard and soft skills they need to do their jobs. However, results have shown that when it comes to retaining skills, experiential learning is most effective.

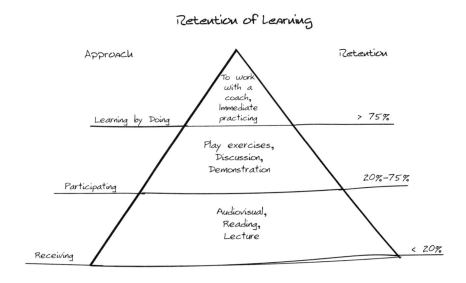

Studies about adult education reinforce this idea and recommend a mix of strategies to build competencies and professional skills. Research also shows that the most effective learning experiences come when organizations look at training and development as a blend of learning opportunities. Experience-based learning on the job can make up to 70% of a person's skill development; 20%

70-20-10 Learning

70% Experience Based	20% Relationships	10% Formal Learning
• Stretch Assignments	• Mentors	• Classroom
• Action Learning Teams	• Coaches	• Teambuilding
• Cross-Functional Teams	• Peer Networks	• eLearning
• Job Rotations	• Performance Counseling	• Conferences
• Community Involvement	• Career Discussions	• Seminars
• Non-Profit Board Experience		• CPA Certification

Learning by doing accelerated his tax expertise.
Mark was a relatively new staff member who accelerated his knowledge base through an intentional and progressive learning program led by an experienced tax partner. To start, the partner invited him to sit in on a client call, listen, and simply take notes. When the two reviewed the notes together, Mark gained knowledge about tax law, understood what he did well, and discovered where he needed to focus. The process continued, and eventually, he wasn't just sitting in on the client calls — he was leading them. He had a similar learning experience when the partner invited him to attend client meetings and followed the same pattern: listen, take notes, review, and repeat. Through this process, Mark progressively added to his knowledge, had more client contact, and was performing at a level much higher than his peers. He's become a supervisor and is following this same process with his younger colleagues — paying it forward.

comes from relationships and knowledge gained from mentors, coaches, and peers. The other 10% comes from formal learning in classrooms, conferences, and other training situations.

There are a number of ways experiential learning helps with staff development. Each day, we learn and stretch ourselves by participating in new client challenges and business opportunities. We gain knowledge through relationships with peers, mentors, and coaches and by networking with other professionals, both internal and external. Developmental experiences are also complemented and enhanced through self-directed learning and more formal and structured training opportunities.

The primary difference between experiential learning and formal training is that the student retains more information by getting involved. Formal lectures or reading assignments are, by their very nature, passive. While a person can learn by reading or listening, they generally will retain and understand much more when they're involved and can interact during the process. The Socratic method is a rigorous question and answer technique that guides active learning through a critical thinking process. See the Appendix for details about using the Socratic method for staff development.

Many partners at Plante Moran say that driving back from a client meeting and discussing that meeting in the car with their colleagues can be a valuable learning experience. We call this "windshield time." Recognizing that the world has shrunk and many staff are working virtually, advisors should look for creative ways to debrief and provide immediate feedback to get the benefits of "windshield time."

At one point, Plante Moran surveyed many of its successful partners and asked them to identify the best practices that would help develop future partner candidates. The interviews revealed timeless factors to support career advancement:

- Future partners were pushed outside their comfort zones with "stretch assignments."
- Future partners were exposed early to partner mentors who became coaches and sponsors for these individuals.
- Partner mentors spent a great deal of quality time with future partners.
- Practice development activities and skill building were emphasized early in careers.
- Real-time feedback was provided on a consistent basis.

- Future partners were open to receiving feedback and acting on it.
- Partner mentors generated a sense of excitement by effectively communicating a shared office or industry vision.
- Future partners worked closely with multiple partners on a variety of projects.

We've learned that advisors who are intentional about exposing their advisees to experiences that will lead to their individual development is part of the secret sauce that contributes to effective staff development. In the Appendix to this chapter, you'll find suggestions for individual meetings and career planning discussions that will aid in creating conversations.

The techniques we've discussed can make the difference in how our staff become well-rounded and multidimensional performers — the basis for a personally rewarding career. Our HR teams will provide a framework, the tools, and the structure for performance management and career planning. However, the best supervisors, leaders, and team partners are those who are good at finding people who need help and providing guidance to those who need support.

When an advisor is focused on developing their staff as individuals, two characteristics stand out, and both are related to communication style. First, the advisor recognizes the importance of asking questions and taking the time to get to know the people they supervise. They'll ask questions and listen to the answers. Second, they'll understand the difference between being a stereotypical "boss" who preaches and an advisor who collaborates, leads, and guides in meeting the goals of the team. Rather than fostering a supervisor-subordinate relationship, they'll be mutually supportive because they're focused on the same goal — recognizing talent, closing skill gaps, building expertise, serving clients, and creating rewarding careers. There's a reason why the word "employee" is losing favor in so many engaged workplaces: The word "employee" connotes that you are working for someone, not working with them as a fully recognized contributor.

APPENDIX — Chapter 4

Nine proactive career moves for staff members

The following actions will help staff members who want to be proactive about their career development. These suggestions will create opportunities to build individual skills and develop a more engaged relationship with a supervisor.

1. Meet with your supervisor and ask what an appropriate "stretch assignment" might be for you.
2. Travel to and from a client engagement with your supervisor whenever possible to capitalize on "windshield time" together.
3. Debrief with your supervisor after client meetings, covering the following three questions:
    a. How did the meeting go?
    b. What could we have done differently?
    c. What could I do differently next time?
4. Ask your supervisor for feedback related to the three most important things you can do to advance to the next promotional level.
5. Invite your supervisor to breakfast or lunch. Use this time to discuss client or career issues. Come prepared with a list of topics to discuss regarding client work, technical or career issues.
6. Be open to performance feedback. Focus on how you can use the feedback to improve (rather than being defensive).
7. Seek out opportunities to work "elbow to elbow" on the job with your supervisor.
8. Seek out opportunities to work with multiple supervisors.
9. Request a speaking role at an upcoming client meeting and rehearse in advance with your supervisor.

Career discussion meetings

We offer the following tips for individual meetings with a staff member. These can be tailored depending on the situation — a formal performance management or career planning discussion, or a meeting between mentor and mentee. Use these to stimulate your thinking and create a meeting that best fits you and the staff member you are helping to grow and develop.

Preparation for career discussions
- Gather facts.
- Gather feedback from others who have worked with the individual.
- Make a list of questions and/or observations.
- Prepare an outline.
- Refer to your notes from previous meetings.
- Remember to deliver fact-based observations, not opinions.
- Candor is kindness.
- Anticipate how your advisee will react to feedback, both positive and negative.
- Be prepared to offer solutions for observations you will make.
- Select the proper setting and the appropriate timing for the meeting.

Meeting tips
- Set the stage for a collaborative conversation.
- Build rapport, confidence, and trust first (see potential questions below).
- Ask leading questions that allow the individual to self-evaluate on their accomplishments and areas of focus and improvement.
- Ask for/give specific examples/options. Deliver fact-based observations.
- Don't merely focus on forms.
- Don't directly compare staff to their peers.
- If a number of messages will be delivered, consider deposits to emotional bank account before addressing emotional bank account withdrawal items — this maximizes the likelihood of listening.
- Be aware that everything you say, even off-the-cuff remarks, might be perceived as important to those you're training.
- Avoid complaining about how busy you are. If you take a step back to count your blessings, it will put everything into perspective.

Questions to ask
- How do you rate yourself on an overall happiness scale — right now — of 1 to 10? Keep track over time.
- What's the best thing you did this year/last six months? Personally and professionally?

- What might you like to change regarding the past six to 12 months?
- Where would you like to concentrate some of today's discussion?
- Describe a great day for you.
- What are your greatest strengths/areas for improvement?
- What have you liked/disliked about your recent assignments?
- Have you identified your specific area of focus?
- What experiences would you like to have that you haven't had yet? What's realistic?
- What's your biggest challenge with your career? How can I/we help?
- What impacts your stress level, positively and negatively?
- Consider a "day in the life" for younger staff members or ask if there are specific experiential learning opportunities that may be desirable (client meetings, contact sessions, etc.).
- How well are you balancing your various obligations?
- Where do you see yourself in three to five years?

Individual action plans — goal setting and follow-up
When advisors and advisees set action plans, it's important to have agreement on the specific goals and action steps that will target the desired behaviors. These should be practical and apply directly to the work setting.
- Make sure goals are realistic.
- Set concrete steps to reach these goals — design each step necessary to reach the vision and the criteria for success.
- Hold advisees accountable — they are responsible for their own development and advancement.
- Look back and pay it forward. Review last year's performance and focus on next year's goals in the same meeting. That's more productive and inspirational than just measuring accomplishments.

Following are some potential goal-setting areas to recommend for individual action plans, depending on the behavior that is being targeted.
- Network development/foundation
- Expertise development
- Experiences

- Projects that stretched you
- Additional reading to create depth and breadth
- Volunteered for something different
- New way to enhance your balance
- New idea shared with others
- Difficult conversation (led or participated)
- Suggestions regarding how firm/practice area should evolve or change
- Have you mentored/helped a less experienced staff person?

Difficult conversations

Inevitably, there will be times when you must deliver a difficult message to a staff member. When low or unacceptable performance is the issue, be sure to consult your HR contact for advice and direction.

- Deliver the message in a fact-based manner using clear words. Do your best to eliminate opinions and minimize emotion.
- Create context.
- Words matter — avoid inflammatory words like always/never.
- Listen to the response. Don't rush the conversation. Allow for reaction.
- Ask the recipient to repeat what they heard.
- Seek clarity — discuss solution options/ideas.
- Consider whether a second person should sit in on the meeting.
- Consider asking for a written summary within 72 hours after the meeting to confirm what they heard.

Using the Socratic method

Advisors may be familiar with what educators call the "Socratic method." This teaching technique allows a teacher to help a student understand a problem by thinking it through critically. By asking the student a series of well-tailored questions, the teacher can assist the student in learning a concept actively rather than passively. This method of inquiry is known in several fields, perhaps most commonly in the teaching of law. Law professors routinely single out a student to answer a series of questions about a case they've read, tailoring the questions to force the student to think about the issues raised and to reconsider any positions they may have taken previously.

With individually focused staff development, an advisor can lead an advisee on a similar path of inquiry to resolve issues arising in the workplace. An advisor can ask questions of an advisee and "drill down" to the critical points by asking the questions that define the issues at hand and might not even need the answers to be given for the staff member to reach a solution. It may be a time for empathy, candor, or both.

Here's a sample that addresses work-life balance options that you could consider. Keep in mind that a given answer to a question may lead to an unexpected direction, so it's imperative for the advisor to listen to the answers carefully, paying close attention not just to the answers given but, when possible, to what the staff member is really saying. It's impossible to teach emotional intelligence or empathy, so this process may take time for both the advisor and the staff member to become adept at it.

The staff member may say, "I'm working too much, and I can't seem to get everything done at work...or at home."

Question: "How much are you working? Do you know how many hours you're working?"

Many staff members will respond to that with something like, "I'm not sure," simply because they feel overwhelmed. They're worrying about work when they're at home and vice versa.

Potential follow-up questions could be: "Have you prioritized what you have to do? Are you focused on the right things at work? Are you getting everything completed, or are too many tasks being left close to completion but incomplete?"

"I'm doing everything I am asked to do."

Other potential follow-up questions:

"How about we go through it together? Should you be doing all of these items? Are these your priorities or someone else's priorities? Could you delegate some of these tasks? Are you involved in the right things or are you working at the right level?"

This line of questioning will help the staff member narrow the focus of the issue and zero in on what's causing the problem. Perhaps the staff member needs to examine how many hours of billable time they're spending compared to non-billable hours. What's the ideal targeted mix? Perhaps they need to examine their support team structure and learn to use their team more efficiently. Or perhaps they need to figure out how to attract more support staff or simply help the staff member set the correct priorities for their team. A staff member can help set priorities and manage expectations for those with whom they work.

An advisor can assist a staff member in figuring out what their "personal" team structure should look like and how they might delegate some of their tasks, and they can help them optimize the number of hours they work by delegating, shifting, or sharing some of their tasks (see Chapter 6: Delegation). Sometimes, the staff member needs to learn to say "No" from time to time when being asked to assist with more assignments.

Question: "How are things going at home?"

"I don't have enough time there either."

Question: "Are you doing everything yourself? Could you hire someone to take care of the cleaning or yardwork?" (Help them pinpoint what's causing the pressure at home or whatever tasks they have that take time away from what they really want to do, like spend time with their family.)

Many staff members are convinced that work itself is the problem. They feel their workload cannot be lessened and that any attempts to lighten it would reflect poorly on them. Yet, quite often, the problem of feeling overwhelmed can be resolved by breaking the facts down and defining the issues. Often, staff members just need direction, and an advisor can provide it by walking the staff member through the problem in a logical, unemotional manner.

Sometimes, the questions lead to answers the staff member might not have thought of — or might not have considered possible. Would the advisor really allow a staff member to seek help on projects without thinking less of them? Does the advisor really care about the staff member's home life? The answers to the questions may or may not lead to a solution, but simply asking the questions may also lead the staff member to bring a clearer picture into focus.

"The delicate balance of mentoring someone is not creating them in your own image, but giving them the opportunity to create themselves."

—Steven Spielberg

"Show me a successful individual, and I'll show you someone who had real positive influences in his or her life. I don't care what you do for a living; if you do it well, I'm sure there was someone cheering you on or showing the way. A mentor."

—Denzel Washington

CHAPTER FIVE

Mentoring - The 1:1 relationship

The following scenario will be familiar to many experienced advisors: You walk out of a client meeting with a staff member who's wowed everyone by presenting a complex project to a very satisfied client. When asked for their reaction to the meeting, the staff member is far from enthusiastic. Their ho-hum response: "I've handled projects like this so many times. I know it went well, and I should be more excited — but it all starts to feel the same after a while." Clearly, this is someone who's looking for more.

This lack of enthusiasm shows a staff member at a career crossroads. They want to move to the next step, but they may not be able to see it. They may even question if there is a "next step." A staff member in this phase of career doldrums is a prime candidate for the dedicated guidance of a mentor. The disciplined help of a mentor could mean the difference between lackluster engagement and fully charged performance.

A mentor's role is to provide individualized guidance to their mentees — literally to help move them from point "A" to point "B." Today's mentoring is

Why the apprenticeship model works
In the apprenticeship model, the master craftsman and the apprentice work side by side. The master guides the apprentice in his or her learning, offers critiques and mentorship, and guides his or her learning by working "elbow to elbow."

designed to deliver the same outcomes that the apprenticeship model has delivered to trades since the Middle Ages. Under an apprenticeship, a novice would spend years with a master craftsman receiving one-on-one guidance in an immersive learning environment. In both apprenticeships and mentorships, the novice gains from the experience and dedicated guidance of their teacher.

The roles and functions of a mentor are as varied and numerous as there are types of people. As a result, no two mentor-mentee relationships will be the same. These relationships differ from the typical employer-employee/supervisor-staff relationship in that the guidance and counsel delivered are above and beyond the usual staff development that might take place. Mentoring is a supplemental experience, and it begins with a mentor who's willing to contribute and a mentee who's willing to learn. The mentee's willingness to learn is essential. It takes two to create a productive relationship.

Mentorships can be created in a variety of ways
Most advisors will be able to sense when a person is in need of a mentor. It may be a staff member at a career crossroads or one who's confused about their future. The staff member with waning enthusiasm described earlier in this chapter is an example. A supervisor may recognize a staff member who could benefit from the assistance of someone with more experience. Or it may arise naturally, when a more experienced staff member takes a less experienced person under their wing. In some organizations, there are individuals who could be considered "power mentors" because so many people gravitate to them. On the other hand, some staff members who are

The value of informal interactions with a mentor.
Gavin recalls how his mentor took advantage of informal situations to build rapport. "He'd sit down and ask a general question. It would get me energized, and the conversations flowed from there. Those informal touches and spontaneous interactions really helped me, and they didn't take a lot of time. Having those kinds of conversations is where the real magic happens."

struggling may simply benefit from having a "buddy" they can turn to for help. One leader who benefited from a mentor and is now mentoring others said, "Mentoring is effective when it's needed and not just on a schedule. It can be informal lunches, phone calls, or face-to-face meetings."

Some mentorship programs may be formal

At times, an organization will create a formal mentoring program to address specific issues facing a group of their staff members. For example, Plante Moran initiated formal mentorship programs for members of its tax team and also to provide career direction for female staff at a critical juncture in their careers. The impetus for creating a formal mentoring program can arise when the organization recognizes it needs a strategic initiative.

The right mentor

As an advisor who recognizes that your staff member would benefit from a mentor, your role will be to find the person who best fits their needs and who can help them successfully jump over career hurdles. Depending on the career goals of your direct reports, that person may or may not be you. A mentor working with someone in a different department, practice area, or outside the organization could help staff members think differently, find creative solutions, and understand the bigger picture. Imagine the dynamic synergy that happens when a linear thinker is matched with a mentor who brings a broader field of vision, and vice versa. Plus, the mentee may feel more open and relaxed than they would if the mentor were their supervisor. In addition, a mentor may be more candid with a mentee who works in a different part of the organization. Whoever the mentor is, they need to be a good judge of potential in others.

The mentor-mentee relationship

The relationship between the mentor and the mentee requires both parties to be fully invested and committed to the relationship. While the mentor contributes knowledge, experience, exposures to specific opportunities, and feedback, the mentee contributes hard work, experience, study, and the willingness to ask questions and be receptive to feedback. Both parties work together and share open communication and trust.

Mentor/Mentee Relationship Continuum

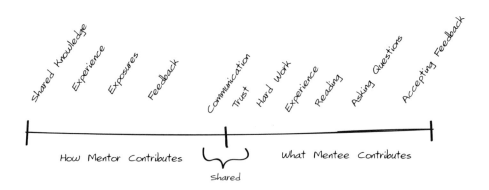

How Mentor Contributes | Shared | What Mentee Contributes

A few words about accountability

Here's my definition: "Accountability to a plan doesn't make us less professional, less caring, or less flexible. It defines success, calibrates results (versus measuring effort), creates opportunities to celebrate, stimulates teamwork, creates focus, and allows us to optimize our efforts. All delivered in moderation." Accountability doesn't have to be onerous or challenging, but the goals have to be clear. Otherwise, how would you know when you have achieved them?

Mentoring: Not babysitting

The mentor-mentee relationship will evolve over time, but it relies on honesty and candor. Mentors should be cautious so as not to be either overly harsh or too nurturing. While their role is to help the mentee, they're not a babysitter. The mentor should set the right standards, making sure the mentee knows they're not expected to know everything or to do everything perfectly the first time. Here are additional mentoring guidelines that enable trusting communication and actual progress for the mentee.

- The mentor should be transparent in the relationship.
- The mentor should recognize the right time to offer key advice.
- The mentor should recognize and articulate gaps in the mentee's experience or knowledge and suggest the right experiences to fill those gaps.
- A mentor shouldn't be afraid to ask the mentee to stretch. It's up to the mentor to know which opportunities are appropriate for a mentee who's ready to be stretched outside their comfort zone.
- The mentor and mentee should work together to set a realistic career goal that takes them from point "A" to point "B." Once a goal is established, they should agree about the specific steps and both understand that the mentee will be held accountable.

Mentoring can be initiated at various stages along a person's career. The Shooting Star mentioned previously might not benefit as much from a mentor early in their career but might gain from one later as their career levels off. On the other hand, a Late Bloomer might benefit from a mentor earlier in their career as they gain their footing.

Advice from an experienced mentor.
It's important to establish ground rules from the beginning in the mentor-mentee relationship. For formal meetings, the mentor should ask the mentee to set the agenda and summarize their notes afterward. This discipline is good for mentor meetings and formal performance management or career planning sessions. To make sure the messages are clear, I ask the mentee, "What are you going to go home and tell your spouse about our meeting today?" Their answer is a good indicator of whether or not what I intended is what they understood.

Help new hires from day one
Starting a new job is unsettling for anyone. New hires often wonder what to say or do in their first weeks and months on the job. Make sure to offer ongoing learning and mentoring from the beginning. New staff members should not feel "new" much longer than it takes to walk in the door their first day on the job. This can establish loyalty early on and help minimize turnover.

From *Succession Transition*

Creating an individualized superstructure for long-term career growth

A mentorship relationship is, by definition, individualized staff development, especially in how a mentor can guide a mentee who wants to take concrete steps forward and create a long-term plan. This type of planning is future-focused and often involves envisioning someone's ultimate career goals. For people who have reached a point in their careers where they can see five, 10, or 15 years out, a tool like the Sustainability Pyramid can help.

The Sustainability Pyramid depicts the necessary building blocks that an organization may focus on to achieve long-term growth and stability. The attributes outlined in the Sustainability Pyramid are the same ones that an individual can incorporate to plan their own long-term and flourishing career. As they work with supervisors and mentors along the way, they can deliberately build a personal superstructure that incorporates the skills, support system, and personal qualities necessary to achieve their career

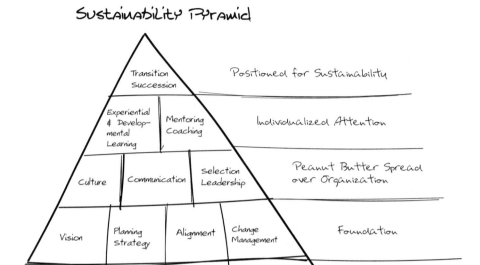

Sustainability Pyramid

Transition / Succession — Positioned for Sustainability

Experiential & Developmental Learning | Mentoring Coaching — Individualized Attention

Culture | Communication | Selection Leadership — Peanut Butter Spread over Organization

Vision | Planning Strategy | Alignment | Change Management — Foundation

goals. An individual who applies the Sustainability Pyramid to mark their career progress is adopting a long-term plan, one that may take years to achieve.

When you think about how stable pyramids are from an architectural perspective, a pyramid structure is an ideal shape to convey the requirements for organizational (and individual) stability. The Sustainability Pyramid comprises 10 components that create a strong organizational system, from its foundation to its ability to transfer leadership through an intentional succession process. Look at any successful enterprise today, and it will be grounded in these fundamental principles, systems, and processes. Conversely, if any of these attributes is missing, the organization may experience some difficulties. The illustration at right depicts the potential result if any of these attributes are missing.

Individuals can use these same 10 components to build a sustainable superstructure for themselves, their colleagues, and their teams. If you're an advisor using this methodology with a mentee, it's important to spend time defining each of these attributes and how they function for the individual. Beginning with vision, this would include a picture, words, or personal brand —whatever a person uses to communicate their perspective for their future. A person with a clear vision knows what they want to accomplish for the long term. A wealth manager may want to work with high-net-worth clients

Sustainability Process and Unwanted Impacts

10-Step Process	Impact
• Vision	• Confusion
• Planning/Strategy	• Uncertainty
• Creating Alignment	• Inefficiency
• Leading/Promoting Change	• Hesitancy & Resistance
• Creating the Environment	• Potential for Chaos
• Communication	• Frustration
• Selection/Leadership	• Inadequate Resources
• Developmental & Experiental Learning	• Lack of Preparedness
• Mentoring/Coaching	• Dissatisfaction & Disappointment
• Transition/Succession	• Ill-equipped for Sustainability

If the process step is missing, then expect the corresponding impact

or their family offices. A senior manager may see themselves as a partner in the firm working with private equity companies. Whatever the vison is, it should include specific and concrete plans, which is where planning and strategy come in. Strategy combined with planning helps eliminate uncertainty. The strategy will include differentiation, how to leverage your colleagues and include them, and ultimately the creation of actionable plans to accomplish the vision.

Alignment, the next attribute, means the staff member is aligned with the goals of the overall organization and in league with the right team members who have a shared understanding and are focused on the same objectives. Imagine what would happen if a mentee's vision and strategy were for a practice area that wasn't part of the organization's plan because it didn't offer sufficient market potential. Time spent developing this practice would be time wasted. Alignment minimizes inefficiency. Finally, the ability to deal with and embrace change is necessary when the inevitable disruption occurs. Disruptions may be technological, regulatory change, people issues, and so on. You may not be able to guess what they'll be, but you can be sure there will be disruption.

The top six building blocks of the pyramid — culture, communication, selection, experiential and developmental learning, mentoring and coaching, and transition/succession — are also required attributes for an individual, especially one who's at a career crossroads. Together with a mentor, they can confirm whether they're in the right environment. Are they a good match for the culture, and is the culture one that will appreciate and support them? Are they on the right team? Are they doing work that fits their interest, talent, and passion? This will call for good communication, which, naturally, sits squarely in the middle of the pyramid. Selection and leadership are next, especially for staff members who are looking for leadership roles in their careers. Perhaps the mentor can identify a leadership opportunity or an experiential and developmental learning assignment, as described in Chapter 4. Leadership also means they'll need the right people to work with and lead, and those people will need to be prepared for the work ahead of them. We'll learn more about this in Chapter 6: Delegation.

Mentoring is one of the final pieces of the pyramid, both for the individual building their career plan and for the people they may lead. The final attribute is succession and transition, which will be activated as the mentee envisions themselves in the role they're striving to achieve and as they build their team for the future. A mentorship program creates the next generation of leaders within an organization. It also fosters stability. If there's an individual who's ready to take over for someone who's leaving, a smooth transition is more likely to follow. Mentorship can help an organization maintain its culture as the "Old Guard" retires and the next generation steps up to take their place. Mentoring may be one of the most effective means to assure that succession isn't accompanied by disruptive change.

Most organizations report that mentoring increases staff retention, and staff members who were mentored report greater job satisfaction. A few cautionary notes are necessary. While everyone may benefit from a mentor, as an advisor, you won't be able to mentor everyone, and it may not be appropriate for you to try. Mentorships won't always work out. There may be a personality mismatch, and changes may be needed. Over a career, you may have more than one mentor, and the lengths of the mentorship may vary as well. A mentor may be there for a career, or they may just be there for a moment in time. Sometimes it's a moment; sometimes it's a lifetime.

Challenging homework from a mentor produced results in the end.

"My most effective mentors were the ones where I was up-front and vulnerable with them," says Jerry, a senior leader in his organization. "When you can be vulnerable, it's a good sign that you're in that relationship. One of my early mentors took an interest in me. He gave me homework, and some of the homework exposed an uncomfortable area for me. Knowing that it was a safe environment, with only my best interests, gave me a lot of comfort. Doing the homework may have been difficult, but it did lead me to succeed in what I was trying to accomplish."

APPENDIX — Chapter 5

Steps to good mentoring
- Help create a reaching vision for a mentee's future career. Don't advocate for an unrealistic career goal or too broad of a goal, and don't allow a mentee to set such goals.
- Create concrete steps to achieve that vision.
- Set specific goals.
- Communicate these goals.
- Focus on goals for the year ahead as well as past performance.
- Get buy-in from the mentee. Successful mentorship programs are driven by the mentee's desire, not the mentor's.
- Don't be afraid to stretch mentees.
- Offer feedback on what someone is doing well, as well as what they need to improve.
- Offer encouragement.
- Hold mentees accountable.
- Conduct mentoring sessions informally and/or in locations that are more relaxed than the office conference room.

Most important reasons for mentoring
- Enhance career development.
- Improve leadership/managerial skills.
- Develop new leaders.
- Put high-potential individuals on a fast career track.
- Promote diversity.
- Improve technical knowledge.

"The really expert riders of horses let the horse know immediately who is in control, but then guide the horse with loose reins and seldom use the spurs."

—Sandra Day O'Connor

"Once you've identified your crucial tasks and sorted out your priorities, try to find a way to delegate everything else. The inability to delegate is one of the biggest problems I see with managers at all levels."

—Eli Broad

CHAPTER SIX

Delegation - A strategic difference

Many firms have someone on staff whose working habits are similar to an individual we'll call "John." John works with seven or eight clients, and he seems to have a full workload. These clients are more than happy with John's work — he's thorough and conscientious and handles the bulk of their work on his own. John is so busy with these clients that he says he's stretched to the limit and can't take on more work. His billable time appears to be at 100% of his capacity, so what's wrong with this picture?

What if John got sick and was out of the office for a period of time? What if John left the firm? Would someone else be able to take over for these clients? What if one of these clients sold their business or engaged another firm? John would have to scramble to replace the work. These events could negatively impact the clients, the firm, and/or John.

Even if John managed to continue his pace with these clients, how long could he maintain his interest in this work without burning out? Doing the same tasks repeatedly for an extended period can grow old for anyone, but especially for someone who's talented. The clients may also miss out on fresh insights they could gain from exposure to other perspectives within the organization.

Another issue to consider is whether John's skills are being used to their fullest extent. Surely, after handling these recurring activities for a long time, he should be in a position to leverage his skills and greatly expand his impact.

This situation is sorely missing delegation. Delegation could amplify John's skills and time, contribute to the development of others, and potentially add some new perspective in serving these clients.

Delegation is more than simply getting someone else to do a task for you. Delegation has numerous benefits for clients, the organization, and individual staff members.

- It creates a variety of experiences for staff members.
- It exposes staff members to new clients and projects.
- It helps generate new ideas and perspectives, which may benefit the client.
- It benefits clients, who reap the value from being served collaboratively.
- It increases new opportunities for staff to learn.
- It increases the leverage of staff members' skills.
- It increases the sphere of influence of the delegator and the number of other staff they impact.
- It creates time for the delegator to do more stimulating things.

Someone in John's position may be in so deep that they can't recognize their need to delegate and the benefits to be gained. Consider this: John is well-versed and efficient with these client situations. With his billing rate of $400 an hour, he has a two-hour task. The benefits could multiply if John delegated a task to someone else who could complete it at $150 an hour and get it done in four hours. The client benefits from a reduced cost, John saves two hours, and a younger staff member learns how to perform a new task. This is a situation where an observant supervisor who can see the big picture could intercede. Sometimes, a gentle nudge (or possibly a strong push) from a supervisor can clear the path for a staff member, especially when that person has never delegated before.

There are multiple reasons why people hesitate to delegate. They may be working too hard and don't take the time to step back, reflect, and plan accordingly. They may be concerned that introducing others to the client may create the potential for mistakes that might harm the client relationship. They may not want to take the time to teach a junior person. How many times have you heard someone say, "By the time I explain it to them, I could have done it myself"? Finally, they might like doing the entire project, because they enjoy the satisfaction of taking a project from start to finish.

Learning to delegate the hard way.
According to Gabrielle, "I was not an effective delegator. I liked to do the actual production work. I got a high level of satisfaction and found it very rewarding. I struggled with the concept of why I'd give work to other people and rationalized around not doing it." She recalls a sobering breakthrough when her team leader told her that others were missing out by her refusal to delegate. "My team leader would tell me to 'give people the opportunity. This is about others, too.' I wasn't thinking another staff member was missing out on a developmental opportunity. As I took on other roles and progressed in my career, I realized there's no way I could have survived and become as productive as I became if I hadn't learned to delegate."

While these concerns may be real, they don't outweigh the positive benefits of delegation. Still, for many, delegation is an acquired taste. Given the level of detail and the importance of making sure work is done correctly, it's natural to want to be involved at every level of an assignment. But delegation allows us to expand our individual role and create the leverage necessary to support personal growth as well as improve the economics of the organization. Delegation contributes significantly to the development of staff, and by not delegating, a staff member may be depriving others of the opportunity for new experiences and to develop and grow more quickly.

Determining what to delegate
Staff members who are so hyper-focused on tasks that they don't have time for anything else may be struggling with issues related to balance. One technique to break the logjam is scheduling the

Delegation Decision Diagram

		IMPORTANCE	
PURPOSE		High	Low
	Burn Out/Heartburn	(C)	(A) Minimize
	Homerun!!	(D)	(B) Quandary Short-term/Long-term Impact
		Low	High
			Passion

- Minimize tasks in the Minimize quadrant – High potential for delegation – Quadrant (A)
- Consider looking for help from a colleague for tasks and competencies in the Burn Out quadrant (C) and consider delegating items in the Quandary quadrant (B)
- Identify and prioritize the tasks and competencies in the Homerun category – Quadrant (D)
- Ultimate goal is to expand your time in the Homerun quadrant and minimize time in other quadrants

weekly personal check-ins that we recommended in Chapter 3. Those check-ins should help them get a handle on what's coming up in their schedule and what could be delegated.

Another technique to use is the Delegation Decision Diagram. A 2-by-2 matrix is one of the oldest tools in the business management world. In this matrix, a staff member sorts tasks and assignments by their importance as well as by how passionately they feel about them. Where a task lands on the diagram can serve as the guide for which tasks should or shouldn't be delegated.

A staff member using the diagram probably wouldn't delegate a high-importance task that they feel passionately about, but what about a task of lower importance and interest? That might be ideal. This exercise will help the reluctant delegator learn how to prioritize and develop their delegation skills as well as grow their self-confidence. After successfully delegating a low-importance, low-passion task, they can then delegate something that is of low importance but high-passion. There are step-by-step instructions to use the Delegation Decision Diagram in the Appendix.

Going through this process, a staff member will need to pay attention to the staff to whom they delegate and how to track their progress. Some staff might require close supervision; others may prefer more independence. A good delegator will learn to adjust to the delegate and help them grow and change as needed.

Delegation requires the delegator to accept a certain level of risk and responsibility. Supervisors who delegate tasks often see an interesting phenomenon. When someone delegates a task for the first time, they're often pleasantly surprised to discover that the staff member not only performs the task well, but they also find a new approach to it, unlike how the delegator would have done it. Sometimes it helps to have a fresh set of eyes look at a task that others may view as routine.

Delegators who are in the early phase of developing this skill can be advised to follow these steps:

- Start small with low-risk activities, and grow the size and scope of delegated tasks. The combination of risk-taking, ongoing involvement, and assessment of your style will best contribute to your success as a delegator and develop your confidence to expand your comfort in this desirable and necessary skill.
- Clarity of communication is a necessity. When delegating a

Delegation vs. abdication.
Henry leads a team with multiple projects on their plate. "When I have a longer-term project on my desk, I don't take it off my list until I know it's handled. I have to remain responsible without actually doing it, and I have to make sure it's done right. Delegating makes me more impactful, but you have to know who you're delegating to. If I assign something to an intern, leave them, and it doesn't turn out right, then shame on me. Sometimes you get disappointed. But sometimes the work product blows your socks off. Delegate, follow up, and check in. It's a constant adjustment based on the circumstances."

task, give clear instructions for the task being delegated. The person taking on the assignment should take notes, and the delegator can ask the delegate to repeat the task back to be sure they understood it.

- Delegation should never elevate to the level of abdication. The delegator needs to remain involved at an overview level and be reasonably available to those to whom they delegate. Schedule timely follow-ups and check-ins with those who are assigned the delegated tasks.

Delegation becomes easier and more acceptable as a staff member gains confidence in the staff with whom they work. Creating experiential learning opportunities and observing staff in these new situations will contribute to that sense of confidence.

Building a personal organizational pyramid

A staff member who's advancing in their career and juggling multiple assignments may be ready for the next step in effective delegation: building their personal organizational pyramid. This process can help staff members evaluate their potential to delegate, and as we'll explain, it's a useful exercise to envision the ideal organizational structure that supports the individual's role within the superstructure of the organization. In John's case, if he develops a personal organizational pyramid, he'll begin to determine exactly how many team members will be needed to complete the tasks needed to serve his client base. He'll have identified a "farm team" that will support his delegation needs. With this insight and some planning, John's assignments could be done by team members at the appropriate level. They'll learn new skills, John's time will be freed up for him to do higher-level work, and the client's needs will be met. John may even gain enough time for other important things, such as business development activities, that may help expand the practice beyond the seven or eight clients he currently serves.

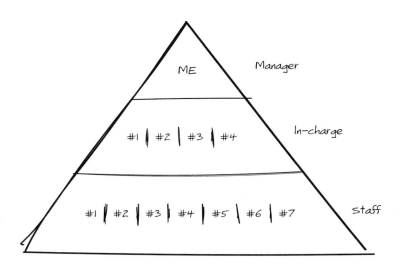

Personal Organizational Pyramid

An alert advisor can recognize when it's time for their advisee to create their delegation plan. They can encourage their staff members to draw an ideal organizational pyramid showing what is appropriate and how many people are needed. The next step is to think about who they would place in those functions, with the knowledge that they won't get 100% of any particular person's time. Since this is the ideal organizational pyramid and not neces-sarily what is totally feasible, there will be gaps because more than likely there won't be enough people, or people with the right skills, to completely populate the pyramid. This exercise enables an in-dividual to identify the experience level and complementary skills that would create an effective and more complete service team.

In John's case, he may envision that he'll need four people at the in-charge level and seven at the staff level. By creating a plan for delegation that includes building a team, John will foster his staff development skills as he begins to understand the people and the skills he needs to develop in others to allow himself to syndicate his knowledge and technical skills. Ultimately, the entire organization benefits from this team approach and resulting skills development process.

When John becomes a successful delegator with a willing team, he'll work to build the personal competencies and skills that increase his confidence in delegating. As a delegator, he'll also have to evaluate his team members and understand when and to whom he delegates. Each person being delegated to may have a different style and require a different approach. Some will want more oversight and day-to-day management, while others might want to be left to handle matters on their own, seeking feedback upon completion of a project. John's staff development skills will grow as he changes his style to fit each person on the team.

The staff member learning to delegate should consider drawing

A leader and advisor discovers the gift of delegation.
Jane, an experienced partner, reflected on her delegation journey. "As a younger partner, I found it challenging to find time to do some of the things that I wanted to do, so I decided to measure what I did in a day using the lens of 'What did I do today that somebody else could and should have done?' The results were eye-opening: At times, 25% of what I did fell into that category. In addition, many of the people on my team that I could delegate to were similarly buried. We worked together to free them up by passing some of their work down to the in-charge level who were probably spending 40% of their time on something that could be done by younger staff. Before I knew it, we experienced the cascading effect of delegation, and we were all spending more time working at the appropriate level. On reflection I realized that I had robbed others of work that was old and routine for me but was new, exciting, and developmental for them."

a personal pyramid for their next promotable position — this is an ongoing exercise that can continue throughout a career. Revisiting their personal pyramid helps the staff member see what gaps may exist and illuminates what kinds of people they need to attract to their team to support the next steps in their career development.

Supervisors should also look for delegation opportunities of their own as a way to cascade their tasks to staff members. A supervisor may observe staff members who are keeping themselves busy — when they ought to be delegating. If you have staff members who look like they are getting into too much routine, coach them to delegate more tasks. This is a great developmental opportunity for them, and it might free them up to help you with tasks you need to delegate. You can create a phenomenon known as a virtuous cycle by modeling good delegation skills and advising your staff members when they can begin delegating to their own personal organizational pyramid. Hopefully they will expand their delegation skills and pay it forward to the next generation.

As a person develops their personal organizational pyramid and delegates more tasks, their billable hours may drop, but their time will still be well-spent as they accomplish more in those billable hours than they did previously.

How to delegate
Start by specifying the outcome you desire to the people you trust to deliver it. Establish controls, identify limits to the work and provide sufficient support, but resist upward delegation. Keep up-to-date with progress, and focus on results rather than procedures. Finally, when work is completed, give recognition where it's deserved.

—*Author Unknown*

How did things end up for John?
John was able to develop a personal pyramid and found many people who could take on the delegated tasks. He was renewed and energized by the new activities he was able to become involved with. His sphere of influence within the organization grew much wider as he was able to take on assignments in multiple offices. Soon he was known throughout the organization, and his personal internal network expanded. He was able to keep the relationships with his original clients, as well as with some new clients, and they all remain happy with him and the work of his team.

APPENDIX — Chapter 6

Delegation Decision Diagram: Step-by-step instructions

Step 1: Identify the major categories of activities you perform in your role and as part of your responsibilities. A few examples — performing compliance tasks, performing (formal or informal) consulting activities, and working on practice development; meeting with clients and referral sources; preparing your billing; gathering and organizing detail information, detail review, overview review, etc. The list can be as summarized or detailed as you like.

Step 2: Categorize these tasks as high or low in importance and purpose. Next, categorize these tasks as high or low on your perspective scale of passion and enjoyment to you.

Step 3: After categorizing, place the activities in the appropriate quadrant.

Step 4: Start with Quadrant A, items that are lower importance, lower risk, and lower interest. Delegate these items first. Remember to delegate, not abdicate. Use these activities to learn how to develop your delegation skills and grow your self-confidence.

Step 5: After you've successfully delegated activities in Quadrant A, begin to become comfortable delegating items in Quadrant B.

Step 6: Give yourself permission to engage a colleague to help execute your high-purpose, low-passion activities (Quadrant C) and develop your skill set in tandem with others. Hopefully these items over time will migrate to Quadrant D.

Step 7: Maximize your efforts to prioritize your high-purpose, high-passion activities to allow yourself to engage in what is purposeful to you. Visualize how you will grow your attention to tasks in Quadrant D to enable you to maximize your time spent doing high-purpose/high-passion activities that in turn will increase your need to delegate more tasks in the other quadrants.

As you go through this process, you will need to observe the staff to whom you delegate and identify how they best receive delegated activities and responsibilities. Identify if they like close supervision or would prefer more independence. A good delegator is able to adjust to the delegate and help them grow and change as needed.

Ensuring that work is done at the right level

In Plante Moran's Statement of Principles, there is a "Principle of Delegation" that reads:

"It is our intent to assign staff members to the level of work that will enable them to utilize their highest abilities over the greatest portion of their working day. This requires that work be delegated to the experience level at which it can be performed most effectively."

Following this approach assures that tasks are being completed at the right level by the individuals who are at the appropriate level to accomplish them. Senior level contributors (and their billing rates) are not mixing in tasks that could be completed by more junior staff members. Clients are being served appropriately and efficiently. The phrase most often used to describe this practice is that each person performs consistently at their "highest and best use."

"It is not necessary to do extraordinary things to get extraordinary results."

—Warren Buffett

"'Would you tell me, please, which way I ought to go from here?' 'That depends a good deal on where you want to get to,' said the Cat. 'I don't much care where —' said Alice. 'Then it doesn't matter which way you go,' said the Cat."

—*Alice in Wonderland,* Lewis Carroll

Business development? Practice development? Sales? Call it what you want, it's everyone's business

Imagine an auditorium filled with staff members from your organization who've come together for the annual all-team meeting. The entire organizational chart is represented — from support staff to senior leaders. When asked for a show of hands to the question, "How many of you want to see us grow by X percent next year?" every hand is raised high. When the next question is posed, "How many want to help with our business development?" more than likely the only hands in the air will be the marketers, the sales staff, and a handful of leaders. While most people recognize the unbreakable connection between growth and business development, few people realize that each one of us has a role to play in both.

Growth is life-sustaining fuel for every organization, no matter its size or line of business. Any company that aspires to thrive over time needs to grow. Throughout this book we've focused on investing in our staff and helping them create rewarding and satisfying careers. All is for naught, however, if the organization doesn't have growth that creates opportunities for these new leaders. In an earlier chapter we talked about the Plante Moran "Wheel of Progress": Good staff –> good work –> good clients –> good fees –> good wages –> good staff. Growth keeps the wheel rolling because it attracts "good clients" and "good staff." (See Wheel of Progress, page 16.)

Some may believe their organization can rely on existing clients to generate all the growth they need, but experience has proven that argument won't hold up for the long term. While delivering additional services (cross-serving) to your existing client base is beneficial to them and to your organization, it's not enough. It's inevitable that some clients will "evaporate" over time. Some may sell their businesses, some will die, and others may, for good and sometimes for unexplainable reasons, change service providers.

Growth is also necessary to provide consistent opportunities for the new leaders the organization develops. In a business structure with multiple owners, it's highly unlikely an organization will achieve a perfect mix of retirements and other departures that would match the increased number of potential new leader candidates. Then there's the inevitable situation when the organization falls on lean times and has minimal or no growth. What happens then to candidates who are ready for leadership roles? How do you retain these staff members you've worked so hard to develop? How do you create an environment that will minimize the possibility of low or no growth in the future?

Bottom line, an organization that intends to sustain itself over time requires focused business development practices geared at attracting new clients or customers. This should be an intentional strategy that's not just for the marketers, the sales team, or the senior leaders: It needs to involve virtually all staff because a long-term, sustainable organization is most effective when everyone has a business development role to play. Your organization may have a formal marketing strategy that includes digital techniques, thought leadership, pursuit strategies, customer relationship management (CRM), and other marketing tactics, but everyone's contributions are necessary to bring these marketing activities to life. Each person's collaboration, whether active or in a support role, can impact the efforts to attract new clients — it's really a matter of matching individual skills with the activities necessary to create demand.

If we ranked the topics where people wished for a "silver bullet" to solve a business challenge, business development would be at the top of the list. While it's one of the most important competencies staff should develop for long-term success, it may be the least understood and the one that provokes the most hand-wringing. Many extremely competent people aren't comfortable "selling" their services to others. *A simple mind shift can change this dynamic.*

If you think about how natural it is to describe your organization and its products or services, you're well on the way to mastering one of the fundamental components of business development — explaining your business, its services, and how it can help its clients. When you build strong relationships across multiple audiences (or "channels" in marketing speak), you're accomplishing another step in effective business development: building connections to potential clients or referrals. Everyone in the organization can learn this fundamental business development skill and execute it flawlessly, whether it's in a social setting or at a community or business event. In fact, this could be considered "Business Development 101," individualized efforts to build awareness and recognition of what the organization does and what it stands for.

The fear factor associated with business development
Business or practice development is a competency that is developed over time, but just the mere mention of it may create discomfort for some. The need to grow the organization and replace the normal attrition and flow of client activity clearly makes practice development a necessary element in the growth and development of every professional.

The value of selling yourself.
"One thing that I wish I'd known much earlier in my career is that business development in professional services is all about selling yourself. Your expertise and the expertise you bring from the firm are the product," says Michelle, a senior leader. This insight came after a rigorous new business pursuit with a well-established company that had worked with a succession of large national firms and was unhappy with their service. "They told us they were wooed into choosing those firms without ever getting to know who would actually be working on their business — and that was a problem. They wanted a promise that our 'sale' was being made by the people who'd be doing the work. That told me that in addition to the firm's capability, we also needed to be able to sell ourselves as individuals, as we were the product, the brand." Michelle made sure their proposal meeting included the staff people who would be assigned to the account and that they were well-prepared to demonstrate their expertise. The owner was impressed by the team and confident knowing who would be doing the work.

Individualized approaches to business development

While the concept that "everyone sells" is widely accepted, advisors face a number of challenges when helping individual staff members build their business development competencies. It's assumed that staff members will be novices in their early years, but they're expected to become more adept as they advance in their careers. In fact, when an individual steps up and expresses interest in participating in business development activities, it's a significant marker of career growth. But as we will see, each individual will build their business development competency in their own way, depending on their personality and personal preferences. Other variables will determine which tactics they use, including their practice area and the type of clients they serve. An individual recipe for success will be composed of the ingredients they choose to use, with a healthy dose of guidance from their advisor.

Even though the approaches each person selects will differ, there are several non-negotiable habits that are necessary, and it's most impactful if these habits are learned early. Simply stated: Practice development skills require discipline, allocation of time and effort, and prioritization. All too often, we see staff members treat business development as an afterthought, something to be done when, or if, there's time. This is understandable, especially in an organization where revenues are based on chargeable time and technical expertise. Tasks that are non-revenue-producing tend to get the leftover effort (if there are any leftovers). It's easy to slip into this habit, so an advisor must hold advisees accountable and ensure they schedule time for business development tasks. If time is an issue, balance (Chapter 3) or delegation (Chapter 6) may need to be addressed. You may want to revisit the concepts in those chapters for ideas about how to help your advisees create time for business development.

A staff member's business development competencies are grounded in a few key building blocks, and it's never too early to begin building that foundation. In fact, if we work on maintaining the skills of the high achievers hired off the college campus and reinforce the importance of these skills from day one, we improve our chances of building future business developers. If we don't, their skills will weaken, and they may even adopt a timid approach based on the influence of others.

While the top priority for a one-to-two-year staff person is learning the technical requirements of their role, their business development efforts may be nothing more sophisticated than establishing a network of college peers for future opportunities and letting their family and friends know where they work and what they do. They'll continue to nurture these initial networks, and in a couple of years, they may have a few referral sources who can be added to their list. There are a number of ways to stay in touch with these contacts, including social outings, networking events, LinkedIn, and even sending them articles that may be of interest. Some of these contacts may stay in their network, and others may fade away over time — that's OK. A network should always be fluid, and it's appropriate to add and remove individuals as circumstances change.

Defining centers of influence vs. prospects.
Business development activities should include connecting with both centers of influence and prospects. "Centers of influence" is an overarching term that describes business advisors that can include CPAs, lawyers, bankers, and private equity personnel, among others. These centers of influence are often the first people companies look to when they're thinking about making a change or looking for help and a recommendation. Staying top of mind with this group can offer many opportunities as they can be great referral sources.

Prospects are businesses that fit the profile that you'd like to win over as new clients. This is not usually a short-term process. It involves getting the opportunity to meet the owner or other C-level leaders, learn about their business, understand their issues, and nurture the relationship until such time that a problem makes its way to the action stage, and they're willing to give your organization a try.

Another way that a staff member in the early years of their career can build their business development muscles is through experiential learning and client exposures, including participation in proposal or pursuit opportunities. Mark's story in Chapter 4: Staff Development is a good example (page 60). Finally, it's important for your staff to become familiar with the services that your organization provides, something that's necessary whether the service offering is complex or straightforward. This includes being familiar with the profile or persona of the organization's "ideal client." (We'll cover more about that in a few pages.) Much of the information about services is available on your organization's website, but you'd be surprised to know how few people visit their own site on a regular basis. (Do you?) Your website is also a good source of thought leadership that demonstrates organizational expertise.

By the time an individual becomes a manager, they'll likely be attending association meetings and possibly giving presentations, participating actively in new proposal opportunities, and proactively fostering relationships in their networks. A staff member at the manager level should also look to identify client needs, offer new ideas and perspectives, and identify additional services that may be helpful to their existing clients. A staff member at this stage should have a formal business development plan of their own that includes specific activities, their time commitment, and defined expectations.

Larry transferred to a new office, and in one of their initial meetings, the office leader asked him for a copy of his business development plan. "I don't have one," he said. "My previous supervisor told me that I was exempt from business development and wouldn't need to do it, which was great news for me because I wasn't comfortable in that role." The office leader responded, "Well, in this office, business development is one of the things we ALL do." Not only did he help Larry strategize his plan, but he also put him in charge of practice development for the entire office. It was a huge focus change for Larry and a major long-term benefit to his career.

We've provided a menu of business development options and tactics for advisors to consider when working with staff members in the Appendix to this chapter. Remember, these are guidelines that will be refined based on the personality and the comfort level of each individual staff member. Stretch goals are good for the long term, and it should be understood that these stretch goals will take a longer period of time to achieve.

There are certain behaviors that apply to everyone, no matter where they are in cultivating their business development competency. An advisor can recommend the following to staff members who are looking for guidance on how to grow:

- Develop an elevator pitch (see Appendix). Practice it with your colleagues and compare notes.
- Ask questions and listen carefully to the answers. Asking questions will serve you well in networking situations and in proposal meetings. By asking questions, you're showing interest in the other person/client, and you're gathering information that will help you understand their needs and serve them better.
- Read (or listen to podcasts) to expand your perspective. Reading makes you more well-rounded and knowledgeable and creates opportunities for conversations. Read about your industry and practice area, current events, your client's line of business, your local sports teams, etc.

Using GYBOOTO to build the business development competency in an office.

An office managing partner wanted to accelerate the business development activities in the office, but he noticed a strong reluctance from the staff. Working with one of the partners, they decided to introduce the GYBOOTO (gee-boo-toe) method to the team. They invited everyone to lunch and delivered a pep talk about the benefits of networking with the assortment of potential referral sources in their community. GYBOOTO would be the answer. Under the GYBOOTO method, each staff person was required to develop a list of attorneys and bankers who worked with their client base. GYBOOTO required them to make an appointment for lunch or drinks with one of these referral sources within the first month and to report their progress by the next meeting. With some reluctance, each of the staff members agreed. As the meeting was adjourning, one of them raised their hand and asked, "What is GYBOOTO anyway? Is this a technique you learned while meeting with one of our association firms?" "No," the office manager replied, "GYBOOTO stands for 'get your butt out of the office.' Now go and make some calls!"

Knowing who you are and where you want to go

As the Cheshire Cat told Alice in *Alice in Wonderland*, if you don't know where you're going, any road will get you there. He could have been talking about the importance of self-knowledge when it comes to business development skills. Without self-knowledge, business development can look like an amorphous challenge with tentacles that can lead to any number of dead ends. But when a staff member is grounded in self-knowledge that leads to a plan, many of the most abstract business development concepts will become more concrete.

There are several business development personalities that most people will identify with. While no two people are alike, individuals can be described as fitting primarily into one of these categories.

- The "Practice-Building" individual is outgoing and enjoys selling, new environments, and meeting new people. They're energized by finding new prospects and new challenges.
- The "Relationship-Focused" individual likes to spend time getting to know others and generally has patience waiting for the right opportunities and the right time for them to be presented.
- The "Technically Focused" person thrives better in a world of definitions and guidelines. They may not enjoy spending time at social functions and meeting new people, but they'll be comfortable making presentations in their area of expertise or meeting people in their field at a conference.

See the Appendix for details about the business development practices that align most closely with these personality types.

Knowing your "Sweet Spot" (discussed in Chapter 3) can also help a staff member develop their business development competency. A staff member's Sweet Spot includes the mix of personal, community, financial, and work-related activities that fit their aspirations. Knowing one's Sweet Spot highlights many of the attributes of the clients they'll want to serve and gives a staff member a head start when they want to narrow down the universe of targets that may be most appropriate for them to pursue. They'll have an easier time targeting potential clients and selecting the tactics that work best for them. Sweet Spot knowledge also will clarify the process of identifying which industry groups or associations to join and which conferences to attend. The same clarity applies to network-building.

If the staff member needs to build a network of referral sources, for example, and their focus is manufacturers, they'll identify the firms and the individuals who work with manufacturing companies.

Using social media for business development.
A senior technology leader who's a social media enthusiast also recommends it to staff members for business development purposes. "Social media helps you build your personal brand and lets your contacts know what your specialties are," says Dev, who favors LinkedIn, Facebook, and Twitter. He encourages staff members to connect with clients and contacts on LinkedIn and to be "active" rather than passive when using social media. "Being active is important," he states, "but be smart about what you put out there because that content will define who you are; it will become your image and your brand." Dev says that LinkedIn is useful to build connections with people you'll meet, for research on business topics, and for syndicating knowledge. "As you use LinkedIn, it will send you articles that reflect your interests. These articles can be shared with fellow staff members, clients, and contacts," he adds. His final piece of advice for those on his team: "I remind them to make sure their profile is professional and narrates what they do and how they do it. It shouldn't just look like a resume."

Developing a "speakable point of view"

In recent years, the concept of "thought leadership" has become a valuable marketing approach, especially in professional services, based on the idea that establishing expertise is a solid way to differentiate your practice or your organization from the competition. Thought leadership is grounded in knowing your client's business and demonstrating recognizable expertise in the issues they face. The ultimate goal of knowing your client's business means the staff person's expertise has developed to the point where they've achieved a "speakable point of view" and can confidently communicate their knowledge and wisdom. The "speakable point of view" that results from knowing your client's business isn't just a benefit to the client — the knowledge and insights are valuable to others who might hire you.

For staff members who want to establish a speakable point of view, their client work is the ideal learning lab to build their expertise (think experiential learning). As demonstrated in the value pyramid, the ability to gather and organize data is the starting point, and technology is driving this data-gathering capability, no matter what line of business you're in.

The process of developing the expertise behind a "speakable point of view" begins with learning and extracting information from data and developing a perspective about it. For example, a staff person may encounter a series of cybersecurity challenges on a regular basis, but their ability to take that information and identify key system weaknesses is evidence that they're developing a distinct perspective about the information in front of them. That staff person

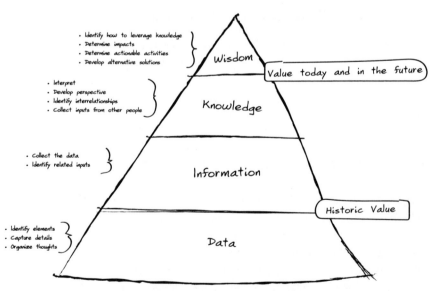

The Value Pyramid

- Identify how to leverage knowledge
- Determine impacts
- Determine actionable activities
- Develop alternative solutions

Wisdom

Value today and in the future

- Interpret
- Develop perspective
- Identify interrelationships
- Collect inputs from other people

Knowledge

- Collect the data
- Identify related inputs

Information

Historic Value

- Identify elements
- Capture details
- Organize thoughts

Data

The best concept of all — know your client's business

may share perspectives with colleagues, clients, or others and use their feedback to inform and expand their perspective. The ability to shape these perspectives and interpret them (and to show inter-relationships with other data points) is evidence that the staff person is becoming knowledgeable. Wisdom is achieved when they understand the circumstances where this knowledge can be leveraged, and they've identified actionable activities and solutions that can benefit a specific client situation. They've developed a valuable "speakable point of view."

As staff members build their insight and advisory skills, these skills can be used with clients and in business development situations. It may include delivering a presentation at an industry group meeting, writing and sharing an article for publication, identifying or helping solve a client issue, or participating on a new client pursuit team. Encouraging staff members to fully develop their expertise and pursue the practice segments that are most fulfilling to them as they grow their careers is invaluable advice.

Tools to support business development

Clients I want to attract

An individual is most likely to be successful at business development when they focus on clients who will appeal to their strengths and things they like. Some individuals might be sparked by complex versus straightforward assignments. Others are driven by the type of people they'll work with or the client's potential for growth. Other common threads that will determine whether it's a good potential client are favorable practice economics, the risk equation that comes with the situation, and the client's good standing in the community. Plante Moran co-founder Frank Moran used to define a good client as "one who is competent in running their business and mature enough to accept advice."

This tool — **Clients I Want to Attract** — will help an advisee identify the attributes of clients they would enjoy serving in the future by highlighting the attributes of clients they have served in the past. It isn't realistic to assume all clients will be ideal; however, this tool allows an individual to isolate the values that are most satisfying for them — a clue for the characteristics they'll want to target in new opportunities. This exercise can also identify areas for personal improvement and the type of colleagues who will add the qualities needed for a well-rounded client service team.

The factors to focus on are the responses listed in columns 5, 8, and 10, which assign a value to the client's "leveragability," relationship strength, and ultimate value to the firm. Leveragability refers to whether you're able to bring additional relationships into the account to expand opportunities. Relationship strength refers to interactions and collaboration with the organization's C-suite. Client value is demonstrated in multiple ways, including whether the client provides reasonable economics, presents a reasonable risk equation, is likely to refer others, and is focused on improvement and/or growth.

Here's an example of how this table might work. Look at the clients with high ratings for leveragability, C-suite relationships, and overall value, and then ask what characteristics these clients have in common. It may be an attractive relationship because the people are open-minded and reasonable to deal with, or it may be that the company has appropriate risk and economics. By focusing on the clients they currently enjoy serving, staff members can use this tool to identify the specific qualities they should target in potential clients. This exercise will also shed light on the companies they should avoid.

Contact contract

A wise person once said, "Constant contact creates constant demand," and I have a personal story to illustrate the truth of that comment. One of our partners challenged me to track new clients I gained over a period of time. He guaranteed that at least 60% of them would be people I had been in contact with in the past 30–45 days. I was skeptical but accepted the challenge and measured my results over the next year. I can report he was more than right — it wasn't 60% of my new clients; it was actually 90% of my new clients! I became an advocate for maintaining continuous contact with prospective clients and referral sources.

Saying it's important to maintain continuous contact is one thing, but doing so is a different story. That's where planning, reminders (visual, if necessary; see Appendix), executing, and accountability can transform good intentions into accomplishments. A reliable and intuitive client relationship management (CRM) tool

Clients I Want to Attract

1 GROSS PRODUCTION	2 NET REVENUE	3 MY HOURS ON THIS CLIENT GROUP	4 LEVERAGE (COL2/COL3)	5 EXPLANATION OF LEVERAGE STATUS	6 REALIZATION (COL2/COL1)	7 RATE 'C' SUITE RELATIONS (A/B/C)	8 EXPLAIN WHY RATING IS AN A, B, OR C	9 EXPLAIN CLIENT VALUE TO FIRM (A/B/C)	10 EXPLAIN WHY CLIENT IS AN A, B, OR C CLIENT	11 KEY APPEALING CHARACTERISTICS

ATTRIBUTES/TYPE CLIENTELE THAT CREATE THE KIND OF CLIENT WORK I WANT TO DO

1

2

3

will be useful — especially if it enables information-sharing across the organization. Some individuals will also benefit from a visual reminder, but that's personal preference. The goal is to implement a plan that holds you accountable. With a "contact contract," a staff member will plan who their contacts are, prioritize how frequently they will contact them, and execute the plan in a timely manner. Ideally, they'll spread these contacts with clients, referral sources, and targets over the entire year and do their best to minimize long gaps between contacts with key people. By adhering to the discipline of a contact contract, the staff person will stay top of mind with their contacts, and a healthy, productive network can evolve. The contact contract plan should be revisited on a regular basis to "upgrade" primary or valuable contacts.

We've been talking about an external network, but it's just as important to create and maintain strong connections within your organization. Contacts between offices, industry, and service groups allow a staff member to build an internal network to support the exchange of information, build camaraderie, identify a source of future and ongoing colleagues, and generally create a breadth of perspective and involvement with a broad cross-section of the organization.

Unique challenges for advisors to help staff build their business development skills

Unlike in the other chapters in this book, advisors may face a unique challenge in this area: coaching and holding staff accountable for skills and activities where they may feel uncomfortable, not well-versed, or as skilled as they would like to be. Some may even feel hypocritical holding others accountable when they themselves aren't doing what we're suggesting. Despite how we'd evaluate ourselves, we owe it to the staff to hold them accountable to execute a business development process that can help the organization win new business and allow the staff the opportunity to demonstrate a proficiency with their business development skills.

We began this chapter by recognizing that many are reluctant to dive into business development and that, frankly, there is no magic pill to substitute for the hard work and discipline required to become good at it. Yet, when we strip away the mystery and stop overthinking it, the basics are simple and fairly low risk, and a lot of the skill comes quite naturally — most people can easily explain what they do and how they help their clients. This simple story becomes the

Business development "homework" produces results for a reluctant advisee.

"My advisor knew that business development was an area where I needed to improve, so he intentionally gave me very specific homework assignments," says Seth, a senior manager who was aspiring to become a partner. "He asked me to come up with 10 questions I could ask when I met someone at a networking event and made sure that I practiced my elevator pitch. We also sat down and went through a list of the top local law firms. He reached out to his contacts at those firms and then matched me up with contacts that I could meet with and develop into referral sources. I committed to a "contact contract" with these individuals, which meant that I'd reach out to them every month or so. Those individuals became professional friends, and now we refer work to each other regularly.

basis of an elevator pitch that can be used in most situations. A staff member's confidence about their business development path expands when they've taken the time to understand where they want to focus; it expands exponentially as they gain expertise by learning from their experience with clients. A practitioner who can speak with confidence and knowledge is an asset in any client meeting or pursuit situation. Admittedly, the discipline required for planning and maintaining accountability to a plan can be a challenge, but it's critical that you ensure intentionality and, at least initially, have someone help hold you accountable to your plan. It's important to figure out what the best individual approach may be and know it will inevitably require stretching your personal comfort zone.

It will take time to grow and develop business development skills. It requires dedication and discipline around planning, selection, and execution. There's no one way to do business development: Your business development approach will be yours alone. It works a lot like the old saying — "The harder I work, the luckier I become."

Summary of business development skills and best practices
- Know the client/industry.
- Know what your organization has to offer.
- Select the right colleagues to work with you.
- Be willing to ask questions and be a good listener.
- Know who you want to work with (for) and why, and then target the clients and contacts who will support your efforts.
- Don't operate in a manner that leads others to view you as a commodity.
- Don't let anyone outwork or out-hustle you.

APPENDIX — Chapter 7

Business development behaviors

The following describes how business development behaviors may progress from entry level to experienced practitioner.

Staff (1–3 years)
- Establishes network of college peers for future business development
- Informs more experienced staff of connections to business development opportunities
- Begins to learn depth and breadth of organization's services
- Updates LinkedIn profile

In-charge to Manager (3–6 years)
- Adds banker and attorney contacts to network
- Helps prepare formal proposals
- Develops working knowledge of other services offered by the organization
- Identifies additional services for current clients

Manager to Senior Manager (6–9 years)
- Maintains network while adding people from associations and community involvement
- Participates in formal proposal process
- Follows through on the sale of additional services based on client opportunities
- Establishes a formal business development plan and goals
- Maintains client satisfaction with current clients
- Effectively differentiates organization from competitors
- Uses practice expertise to develop sales opportunities

Senior Manager to Partner (9–12+ years)
- Significantly builds network
- Takes the lead in formal pursuits
- Attains comprehensive knowledge of other service areas
- Strategically consults with clients on future opportunities
- Understands the role of all players in the buying decision
- Begins to be recognized as an expert in the practice area

Master
- Identifies and executes on opportunities to expand services to current and prospective clients
- Develops effective methods that increase the frequency of opportunities for providing services to existing and new clients
- Effectively "closes the deal"
- Pulls together and coordinates resources to deliver valued services and business results to existing and new clients
- Actively manages a portfolio of decision-makers to create referrals and references
- Can apply knowledge of organization's service offerings within their network
- Syndicates ideas and services to other practice developers
- Broadly recognized as an expert in particular service(s)

Business development topics for advisory meetings
The following concepts can be used in advisory sessions about business development. They will apply to staff members at the appropriate point in their careers. There are multiple options an advisor can use to help individuals develop their competency improvement program.

1. Business development topics and recommended activities:
   - Develop elevator pitch/parking lot story.
   - Make 100 contacts per year — two per week (meetings and phone contact).
   - Network development: Meet and know the individuals who serve the clients you also serve.
     - CPAs
     - Attorneys
     - Bankers
     - Associations
     - Other
   - Keep in contact with alumni and former clients.
   - Visibility: Measure the percentage of time spent in the office vs. outside the office.
   - Focus on allocation of chargeable time — consulting vs. compliance time.
   - Speeches/presentations/articles.

- Promote others, not just yourself.
- Importance of discipline and sticking to a plan.

2. Concepts advisees should understand:
    - Targeting.
    - "If I owned 'This' company, I would…" This is a conversation with everyone on the job, and the purpose is to get people thinking about the client's business. Insights could be shared with the owner as appropriate. This encourages creative thought among all staff; the recommendations don't necessarily have to be technical ideas, either.
    - "Steal the deal" — Figure out how to replicate valuable services with other clients who have similar issues.
    - Client service review — a brainstorming session to identify opportunities that would benefit the client. Participation in a client service review gives staff a holistic review of the client situation.

3. Business development conversations with clients:
    - Ask clients for introductions and referrals.
    - Ask clients what they want/need.
    - Ask questions — for information, to learn, to show interest.

Business development approaches based on the personality types
Approaches for all business developer personalities:
- Establish trust early and maintain it throughout the relationship.
- Remember, it's not about selling; it's about helping and about benefits.
- Find a client or target's pain points and look for ways to make the pain go away.
- Take a holistic view of their organization (e.g., their financial performance, market conditions, competitor activities, strategy, etc.).
- Bring the right colleagues with you.
- Ask probing questions.
- Understand the buying center and decision-making process.
- Communicate periodically with your network when there is no direct agenda around business development.

- Make sure your clients and network know you want more business.
- Always find out specifically why you won/lost business.
- Make a graceful retreat when you determine that a business development opportunity is not a good match.
- Determine if the prospect is a relational or expertise buyer.
- When you lose work, ask the client how they will measure success for this work/relationship. It will add value to their thinking and give you an opening to contact them later to see how successful the work/relationship is.
- Do some self-analysis around why anyone would buy from you, and make changes to create stronger reasons.

If your personality type is a **"practice builder"**:
- Top networkers have, on average, about 20–25 contacts in their networks.
- Figure out quickly who will/won't refer business and prioritize your list accordingly.
- Get the prospect to talk about how they market and sell, and look for insights to turn this into how you can sell to them.
- Ask, "How do you know you're happy with your current provider?" and then keep probing until you create some doubt in their minds.
- Assess your at-bats, size of projects, selection of opportunities, and hit ratio to identify how to improve business development, specifically and intentionally.

If your personality type is a **"relationship builder"**:
- Work and personal life can be effectively intertwined.
- Consider having forums where leaders and/or staff share a cross-selling story.
- If you have served a client for a while, you may be viewed as a purveyor of a commodity. You need to change the relationship to one built on value.
- Always come up with ideas to save enough to cover a portion or all the compliance work/fees.
- Identify 10 things we would do if we were you.
- Account planning for larger, higher-potential accounts.
- Find ways to surprise your client with insights and something of value.

If your personality type is a **"technical resource"**:

- Go to a conference with specific objectives related to business development.
- Get your contact list/network together periodically to share knowledge and to network.
- Reinforce periodically, but consistently, that you are a player in the industry.

Contact contract visual

Following is a visual that illustrates how to plan, prioritize, and implement a contact contract. First, identify the clients, prospects, referral sources, and internal colleagues you want to nurture in your network. Log them into the contact contract. Decide how frequently you commit to being in contact with each person, keeping in mind the seasonality of your assignments, holidays, conferences you will both attend, etc. Add those dates to the chart by placing a circle in the month when you will contact them. Be sure to spread the contact plans throughout the year. Each time that you successfully complete a contact, draw an ⊗ through the circle.

Contact Contract

	January	February	March	April	May	June	July	August	September	October	November	December
Clients	⊗	○	⊗	⊗	⊗	⊗	⊗	⊗	⊗	⊗	⊗	⊗
		⊗			○			⊗				⊗
			⊗					⊗	○			
Targets												
Referral Sources												
Internal Colleagues												

Sample "elevator pitch"

An elevator pitch should be no more than 30 seconds, and it should be a quick introduction to you, your company, and the service or product you provide. There's an abundance of websites that describe the process to create an elevator pitch, and some of them provide templates. An organization will usually have a "boilerplate description" that can be a useful starting point; however, it's always best to tailor the elevator pitch to the circumstance and the individuals who are on the receiving end. The marketing team at the organization can help with this.

The following example of an elevator pitch answers the question, "What kind of work do you do?" by immediately referring to a tough issue their clients face and showing how they could solve it.

"You know how companies face hard times and have cash shortages?

"Well, I advise clients during those situations and develop financial tools to help navigate the uncertainty, the result being that the company has a clear roadmap to success, and its bank has confidence in the company's plan."

"One person can make a difference, and everyone should try."

—John Fitzgerald Kennedy

The Gift of a Career

It's the first day of your new job, an internship during your third year of college. The organization has 60–70 staff members with great clients and leaders who are focused on serving them well. The leaders have committed to fostering an environment focused on each individual, because they see the connection between excellent client service and having good staff to serve them. With this setting and a team of this size, you can imagine how well you might know your fellow staff members. Each person is familiar; you know the assets they offer as a team, their individual strengths and areas for improvement, and their personal hopes and dreams for future success.

Now, roll the clock forward 50 years and envision this same organization. It's still successful and well-respected, and its staff members now number in the thousands. They work in offices, remotely, and across the country. While it's impossible to know everyone, it's more than possible (maybe even expected) to maintain the same familiarity and intimacy with your fellow teammates and colleagues. The intimate organization mentality you first encountered has been replicated dozens of times on multidisciplinary teams across the larger, more diverse organization. Decades have passed, but the rush of familiarity and warmth is still there.

This describes my experience after nearly 50 years at Plante Moran, and knowing how powerful it's been for me and hundreds of others who have built successful careers there, it's this legacy that I've shared in this book. The methods and practices that helped Plante Moran grow can help others adapt to their own work environment.

While we covered many issues, unquestionably there are numerous other details and topics that could have been included in an exhaustive study of what's required to create a "best places to work" environment. But that wasn't my intent.

Rather, my purpose was to delve into those topics that, in my experience, have presented the most frequent hurdles for advisors and leaders who want to create a well-defined, inviting environment that encourages self-satisfaction for people working in a team environment and growth opportunities for the organization as a whole.

Many of us think of our career as a lifelong quest that may or may not always be satisfying or even rewarding. There may be fits and starts, ups and downs — it all varies by individual. But the conditions to create satisfying and engaging careers are achievable no matter the size of the team or the type of the organization. This mindset can grow out of one location or one department and spread to others when they see the benefits it brings for staff engagement, innovation, and productivity. What's important is that the leaders, advisors, and supervisors can make the difference, and it's in their interest — and the interest of the organization — to try. It's an important responsibility, but with the right mindset, a caring attitude, and focus on the individual, it's doable.

The value of one hour

In a world driven by technology, deadlines, and client demands, prioritizing time for reflection — to just think and plan — is difficult, but necessary. Setting aside one hour every week to reflect on what's happening at work, home, and elsewhere is the strongest recommendation I would make for leaders, advisors, and supervisors (don't forget advisees need to do this as well). The agenda for that hour of reflection could include any number of topics, including the open projects and assignments that lie ahead, how and who should be involved, personal balance, the "care and feeding" of the staff in your personal pyramid, or checking milestone progress on personal and team goals.

Ironically, taking this hour will ultimately save time, especially when it reveals opportunities for delegation, staff collaboration, experiential learning, new types of assignments, or positive reinforcement.

A little planning can save a lot of time and create opportunities.

A weekly personal planning appointment can be a valuable way to get us out of autopilot mode. One senior leader had a wake-up call when he was faced with delegating a task that had become a habit for him. He'd never stopped to think about the task and how to improve it until his upcoming sabbatical required him to assign it to someone else while he was away. The task involved numerous steps that had taken several hours to complete. The person who was assigned the task took it on effortlessly, eliminated steps, and improved the process. Upon returning from his sabbatical, the leader continued to delegate the task and was simply provided the weekly summary from then on. When used effectively, the weekly hour dedicated to reflection can produce fresh insights about everyday tasks; opportunities for advisors and advisees could result.

In addition to taking time to reflect, leaders and advisors need to continually ask questions, prioritize options, and make choices. Someone asked what my advice would be for the new leader of a team who is stepping into a supervisory role for the first time. Giving themselves the precious time to reflect and developing the ability to make decisions by asking the right questions are foundational tools. I would encourage them to look at each of their team members with a dispassionate eye. What are their unique talents and their most significant issues? How best to help them grow, learn, and contribute? An objective appraisal will identify their unique talents and will illuminate the path to help them become more effective and achieve their goals. That means candidly addressing their areas of improvement with clear observations rather than impressions. As we've mentioned before, every one of us has, and always will have, areas to improve.

The new supervisor who takes staff development seriously is helping their advisees, the organization, their clients, and themselves. A strong team with a strong foundation creates opportunities and growth for everyone, including you.

Admittedly, the Plante Moran environment where I spent my career may be considered unique. Adopting these approaches wholesale may cause some people to hesitate, depending on their work environment. Many people avoid trying anything different for fear of rocking the boat. However, you don't have to employ every single concept in this book to benefit from these ideas. While every workplace is different, an intentional focus on individuals can make the difference.

To start the process, you may try them piecemeal — even one at a time if that's more comfortable for you — and you should still see positive results and may create some momentum. If you aren't ready to go out and attempt the things described in "Business Development," you may still benefit from the advice in the chapter on delegation. Discussing self-awareness with staff members may be uncomfortable for some, but the lessons in the chapter on balance would still give you value if you consider them. Perhaps take a look at your environment and ask which of the ideas in this book could most easily be applied in your organization, and consider how to begin that process.

You may be pleased to find that individuals you supervise are more receptive than you'd think to some of the ideas in this book. Many of the chapters deal with processes that support advancement and focus on finding the right place within an organization for a staff member. Once a staff member realizes this, they should be motivated to try these ideas — even if it means trying something "new" — and be in a position to pay it forward.

It's worth noting that staff development, as a process, is more art than science. The chapters of this book have lists, guidelines, and suggestions, but virtually everything will be more impactful if it's tailored to the personalities and circumstances of both the advisor and the advisee. And, like any other art, you will appreciate the impact and become more skilled at it as you spend more time on it. I'll leave you with one final diagram for staff development.

To be successful at staff development, you need to be open-

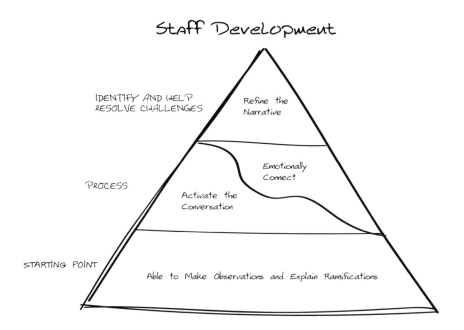

minded and have a desire to help. An open door helps. But desire alone will accomplish little. Start by simply making observations (not expressing impressions) and help staff understand the ramifications of their actions. From there, you'll begin the process, activating the conversation with advisees on the various topics we have covered. Hopefully, that will lead to some emotional connection, which will allow the staff member to connect with the advisor and help them embrace the process. Along the way, the advisor can help the advisee identify and resolve challenges. The narrative will be refined and the path to growth and achievement will become clearer.

Throughout my career at Plante Moran, I often returned to a simple mantra. These three sentences guided me the entire way. I reminded myself that — regardless of anything else — I needed to be:

- Innovative in thought.
- Principled in intent.
- Intentional in action.

Now, go give your staff the Gift of a Career.

((☆))

Sources

A Word from the Author

Jim Collins, *Good to Great: Why Some Companies Make the Leap ... and Others Don't,* New York: Harper Business, 2001, harpercollins.com.

Chapter 1

Work Institute, 2019 *Retention Report,* workinstitute.com.

Chapter 2

Dr. Robert Pasick, Ph.D., and Dunrie Greiling, Ph.D., *Self-Aware: A Guide for Success in Work and Life*, Createspace Independent Publishing Platform, 2016.

Chapter 4

William N. Dember, *"Pacer Theory," The Psychology of Perception*, New York: Holt, Rinehart and Winston, 1960.

Chapter 7

Value Pyramid

The origin of the presentation of the relationship between data, information, knowledge, and wisdom is uncertain. The acronym DIKW is widely used as a shorthand way to connote the hierarchy of the transformation from data to information to knowledge to wisdom.

Index

L

Late Bloomer 5–6, 75
LinkedIn 1, 99, 103, 110

M

Mentor/Mentee Relationship Continuum 74
Millennials 1, 3, 14–15
Moran, Frank 105

N

Network 28–29, 34, 41, 58, 65, 91, 99, 103, 108, 110–111, 113–114

O

One-size-fits-one 51

P

Pacer theory 57, 123
Pasick, Robert 11, 24–25, 123
Personal ecosystem 40
Personalized development 1–2
Personal organizational pyramid 88–89, 91
Practice builder 113
Principle of Delegation 93
Problem solving 28–29, 34, 57
Professional Services Professional Development 53
Prospects 99, 102, 114
Pyramid of Progress 54–56

R

Relationship builder 113
Re-recruiting questions 19, 21, 44
Retention of learning 59
Risk-taking 47–48, 87